Miracles or Coincidences

Miracles or Coincidences

Miracles do Happen

Geraldine Moran

DISCLAIMER

All the information, techniques, skills and concepts contained within this publication are of the nature of general comment only and are not in any way recommended as individual advice. The intent is to offer a variety of information to provide a wider range of choices now and in the future, recognising that we all have widely diverse circumstances and viewpoints. Should any reader choose to make use of the information contained herein, this is their decision, and the contributors (and their companies), authors and publishers do not assume any responsibilities whatsoever under any condition or circumstances. It is recommended that the reader obtain their own independent advice.

First Edition 2010

Copyright © 2010 by Geraldine Moran

All rights reserved. No part of this publication may be reproduced, stored in a retrieval system, or transmitted in any form or by any means, electronic, mechanical, photocopying, recording or otherwise, without the prior written permission from the publisher.

National Library of Australia
Cataloguing-in-Publication entry:

Geraldine Moran, 1963
Miracles or coincidences : miracles do happen / Geraldine Moran.

1st ed.
ISBN: 9781921630323 (pbk.).

Miracles.
Coincidence--Psychic aspects.
Coincidence--Religious aspects.

202.117

Published by Global Publishing Group
PO Box 517 Mt Evelyn, Victoria 3796 Australia
Email: info@TheGlobalPublishingGroup.com

For Further information about orders:
Phone: +61 3 97361156 or Fax +61 3 86486871

ACKNOWLEDGEMENTS

When writing a book there are many people who go into the final product. They may help through their enthusiasm, through their suggestions, through their interest or through the hands on role they have in its production. In order to be at this point and acknowledging people who have helped there are literally a cast of thousands. If your name doesn't appear, don't fret, I am thinking of you and would welcome the reminder that I forgot to add you to the list. So here goes.

To my true love Geoff, I really am blessed to have you in my life to show me the greater point of why we are here. To Bella, who we patiently wait to come into our lives.

To my family, who have at times wondered, thank you for your patience and acceptance.

To the people who have had the physical responsibility in getting the book published I firstly want to thank Deb, who was my master coach and mentor. She showed me what courage means and how to keep going, step up and never give up. She also highlights what it is to be a great person. Thank you.

To Jo and Darren and all at Global Publishing, a huge thank you for your patience and assistance; to Daryl and Andrew Grant for taking the time to encourage and guide by just being themselves; to my fellow bestseller authors – thankyou; to Belinda www.bdabooks.com.au who did a great job with editing and to Rebecca www.infinitecommunication.com.au for her fantastic press release and encouragement.

To Narelle, thanks for the fantastic cover and design. www.ngirldesign.com

To Andrea and Ren thanks for the transcription.

To the people who share the pages with me and who gave of themselves through their stories, I am truly humbled and blessed to have had the opportunity to speak with you and to learn more about the amazing journeys that we share. To Paul, for being a wonderful mentor who exudes love for his fellow man; to Pat for being a constant reminder of what forgiveness can bring into your life; to Paul for showing the courage to keep going in adversity. Thank you Vince and Marie for sharing your stories and being inspirational; to Tracy for miraculously showing up at the Angel of the North and sharing her amazing life story; to Michael for sharing his memories of an amazing experience and for going on to help others on their journey with serious illness. And lastly, but by no means least, to Kerrianne for providing a truly moving and wondrous insight into our country, its ancestors and our future– that is deadly.

I want to send a special thank you to my friends and fellow trainees at Beyond Success, they really showed me how to grow. Thanks also to Mary, Julie, Emma, Caius, Kathy and Andrew. To Jason, Steph, Mick, Nick, Carolyn and everyone who works as crew, thank you.

A special thank you to Kat and to Jules who helped find the me who is a great friend, thanks for showing me that and for being great friends to Geoff and me.

Thanks to Michelle for her friendship and enthusiasm. Thanks Karen, Ange, Gus, Ange, Michelle, Monika, Marilyn and Michael and Gail, Pam, Sandy, The R& N girls and Donna and Gail..

Thanks to Robert and Michael, for viewing the manuscript and sharing your thoughts and ideas.

Thanks to Pam for all her help. www.dare2bemore.com

Thanks to Claire Morris for her marketing ideas.
www.kandooonline.com.au

I also want to thank Geoff, Dayna, Peter, and Justine for the mastermind encouragement.

Love and Light to all

TABLE OF CONTENTS

Foreword – Dr John Demartini	1
Introduction	7
M – Mastery of the Mystery	17
Paul Blackburn's Thoughts on Miracles	27
I – Invite the Infinite Intelligence of Our Invisible Soul	43
Pat Mesiti's Thoughts on Miracles	53
R – Recognise Results and Mould Your Reality	61
Paul Barratt's Thoughts on Miracles	73
A – Attitude of Gratitude	93
Michael's Thoughts on Miracles	103
C – Centering – Become the Captain of Your Soul	117
Kerrianne Cox's Thoughts on Miracles	131
L – Limitless Power of Love and Light	159
Marie and Vincent Ang's Thoughts on Miracles	169
E – Emotional Mastery	187
Tracey Fletcher's Thoughts on Miracles	199
S – Seven Steps to the Slipstream – Spirit	215
Profiles	227

Foreword – Dr John Demartini

FOREWORD – DR JOHN DEMARTINI

You may be asking yourself right now, what exactly is a miracle and can one truly exist or happen? Is it simply something unexpected, improbable or statistically unlikely? Is it something sacred, divine or supernatural? Does it transcend the laws of nature, or is it only an amazing biological or phenomenal expression of the laws of nature? Is it only something wonderful, fortuitous and beneficial, or could it be that unexplained event which simply beat the odds and appears coincidental to those that remain unaware of the great, underlying and inspiring laws of the universe?

You will have to draw your own conclusions to these mystery questions as you peruse the potentially life changing pages that follow. To me, the very existence of life itself could be considered a miracle. In our vast universe of quantum and astronomical events our very existence and human experience could be worthy of such terminology? Is it not miraculous that the simplest cells emerged 3.9 billion years ago even though the greatest Nobel Prize winning minds on earth have collectively not figured out how? Is not the very diversity of life that has filled every conceivable niche on earth an expression of the truly miraculous?

As Rabbi Avigdor Miller once put it *"All of nature and of science stems from the knowledge that the world was made by a super intelligence. Every object in nature is of endless wisdom no matter how deeply you'll fathom the profundity of a natural object, you'll never be finished with the miracles of plan and purpose that unfold before your eyes. The deeper you delve into it, the more you see how little you know. Everything is so planned, so perfectly set out to serve a purpose, and the purpose is served with the minimum of expenditure of effort. There are millions upon millions of examples of God's wisdom in the world, and each one is a miracle in itself."*

Are we not immersed in daily wonders which are often too pure and intricate to fully behold? Are we not unconscious witnesses of moment to moment miracles living within our amazing and intricate bodies, within our immune reactions, cell divisions and genetic reproductions, though they often lie hidden from our outer perceptions? Aren't our very daily synchronous occurrences amazing expressions of the miraculous? If we explored our lives more deeply couldn't we become awestruck by the magnificent timings of the many complementary opposites that occur in the simplest and most profound aspects of our daily lives?

Could unexplained healing "miracles" be expressions of some immutable and immortal laws applied to our mortal bodies? Could these extraordinary and astonishing happenings be attributed to the presence and action of an ultimate or divine organizing power – or possibly a divinely intelligent matrix of mathematical beauty, elegance and order?

Could the many extraordinary and synchronous occurrences in our daily lives initiate within us a cause for wonder or a pause for astonishment though they could also be considered inexplicable by normal standards? Because that which is normal and usual is considered natural, could unexplainable miracles be considered "super" or at least "epi" natural events? Does the significance of a miraculous event point to the presence or activity of a greater organizing, intelligent or divine power? Could a miracle also be called a sign and signify and indicate something essential or noumenal beyond the existence of the phenomenal?

As the philosopher Immanuel Kant explained the phenomenal world may be an expression of power and that the source from which this power comes could only be the noumenal world beyond. Could energy or spirit without matter be expressionless and matter without spirit, be motionless?

Could extraordinary, astonishing or miraculous occurrences be considered religious phenomena when they express, reveal, or signify a religious reality, however defined? Are not beliefs in miraculous happenings features of most religions? And are not the incidences of, or beliefs in miracles universal, though their functions, nature, purpose, and explanations variable according to the social, cultural, theological and philosophical context in which they appear. However inexplicable, don't all miracles have an explanation in the sense that they are accounted for in terms of the religious and cultural system that supports them and that, in turn, they are meant to support. Without such an accompanying - explicit or implicit – reason or theory, like the presence, activity, and intervention of such realities as divine intelligences or powers, there would be no miracles in the aforementioned sense, but only lifeless and unexplained phenomena.

Now that a brief introduction to miracles has been shared and a series of intriguing questions put forth, is it possible that by simply exploring your daily life through the eyes governed by the wisdom of your balanced mind and heart, you can reveal and experience many such miraculous events. And could they potentially humble and inspire you if they were fully attended to? In the pages that follow there are many stories, anecdotes and inspiring principles that will express and explore the occurrences of a life filled with daily miracles, those that just might already be happening in your life and those you can become inspired by and certainly grateful for.

Foreword – Dr John Demartini

When you listen to the wisdom of your heart and become guided by the inspirations of your balanced mind or soul you will attune to these daily occurrences, these inexplicable events that can inspire awe and reverence for the magnificence of your surrounding environment and amazing life. This book is for you to gratefully open your heart by so that the miraculous events that surround and permeate your very existence can be felt and known and be used to guide your life to one of true mastery.

Read "Miracles or Coincidences" with an open mind and let it open your heart. You will begin to appreciate your daily life, your true magnificence and your new possibilities for living more fully. You are destined to live an amazing and extraordinary life. With the spirit of the miraculous under your wings you will be able to soar to new heights and see even greater horizons. May your journey into the miraculous of your daily living open your life up to the ever present opportunities that lead you to fulfillment and grace! Your Soul is whispering, your heart is pumping and your higher mind and inner eyes are waiting. Is it not now the time to embrace the miraculous?

Dr. John Demartini

Bestselling author of "Count Your Blessings – The Healing Power of Gratitude and Love"

Introduction

INTRODUCTION

> *"There are only two ways to live your life. One is as though nothing is a miracle. The other is as though everything is a miracle."* – Albert Einstein

People have asked me why I am qualified to write a book on Miracles. My response is always the same. I am nobody special. I am as qualified as you are to write one. Why? Like you, I am a miracle. If we stop to think just briefly about how we are conceived, born, continue to breathe and wake up each morning to see the new day form, isn't that pretty amazing? I am an ordinary human being who sees extraordinary things happen, in my world and to others, and I try to put a name on those things. It is no different from the others who have gone before and written about their experiences and those of their contemporaries. Ultimately, I have a desire to share some thoughts with others, and just perhaps, people may benefit from the words that they read.

Why Miracles? We live in a truly miraculous world. Awesome things happen and we struggle to find reasons and give explanation. I have been fascinated by unexplained occurrences for a lot of my life. I am only beginning to see how they may come about, although their mystery is perhaps their greatest appeal. Why write a book about Miracles today? For many believe that miracles only happen when saints intervene and that this has no relevance in today's world. Today's world is very removed from the traditional religion that even we grew up with. We search for answers outside the walls of a church.

Introduction

For those of us in Australia, the Catholic Church is getting closer to officially canonizing Australia's first saint. I am not Catholic, but for many of my friends and some of my family, this is a very important event in their church's history. In modern times, we still strive to believe in miracles and in something greater than ourselves, and to have this reinforced by some sort of an authority seems to allow people to believe. It somehow legitimates that knowledge for us. A visit to Mary McKillop's Chapel in Sydney is truly a special experience. Does the announcement have any relevance beyond the Church? Many people would say no, but that overlooks the wonderful story behind the Saint and the fabulous outcomes that people have attributed to her long after her death. During her lifetime, she was a remarkable example of getting on with the job and ignoring her critics and detractors. If Australia is to have a Saint, then it's great to think it's one who would stand up to her peers and superiors, follow her dreams and achieve and leave behind her a legacy that still helps countless children and people throughout our nation.

Do you want to know something? We all have that ability. To dream, to achieve our goals and aspirations, to live with our light shining for others no matter what we do. Throughout time, different religions, thinkers and groups have tried to unravel the mystery of our existence on earth and our connection to God. There; I said God. The Gnostics really believe that we each have a divine spark and that it is just waiting for us to ignite it and connect to our divine nature. The Alchemists believed that we could change base metals into gold. I see this as a metaphor for us to change our base nature into the gold of our true selves. It is through this process that we begin to bring miracles into our lives and those around us. For yes, we are all connected and it is almost like we are joining the dots as we each form part of the stories of one another. The players in the stories will change and some will stay the same. Some will have cameos and others will be the leads for a while. We each contribute to the greater whole regardless of our beliefs, our ideals or sometimes even our willingness. So where does all that leave miracles?

Part of our journey of discovering our true nature involves miracles. In finding ourselves, we also find the slipstream that truly leads to remarkable events and occurrences for us. I keep using the word miracle, but what does that really mean? Most days, headlines in the papers refer to a miracle comeback, a miracle goal, a miracle career. Especially in the sports sections. The Concise Macquarie Dictionary (1982) defines a miracle as "an effect in the physical world which surpasses all known human or natural powers and is therefore ascribed to supernatural agency." The word is derived from the Latin "Miraculum," or object of wonder.

So what do I mean when I say we can get to a miracle in 7 steps; that there are ways that we can begin to see these things that are happening everyday around us? We can invoke them in our lives and hopefully this will lead to a better world for us all. It takes a few people to make a change and yet that change can be far reaching. Many brilliant people are, and have been, telling us about such things over the centuries. Saints have been attributed with miracles in their own lives and later, often after their death, in the lives of others. Holy men, from Christ to Muhammad to Buddha, and modern masters like Sai Baba, bring about huge changes for people.

The meaning for us today is also being carried by great speakers, thinkers and authors. Wayne Dyer, Deepak Chopra, Dr John Demartini, Loral Langemeier and Louise Hay are all making contributions on the world stage. Great Australians like Paul and Mary Blackburn and their team at Beyond Success, Pat Mesiti and his team at Millionaire Mindset are really distilling a way for people to bring that magic into their lives. They, together

Introduction

with Dr John Demartini, have led me to write a book that I have long dreamed about but never really had the connections or understanding to write. The shared knowledge and sharing of their wisdom helps countless people and I am not different. I just happened to want to write a book which would spread that wisdom and offer practical ways for people to change their lives.

Since starting this book, I have found many people have gone out of their way to help me and to encourage me. Not the least are Andrew and Daryl Grant, who show what two ordinary Aussies can achieve in starting and building an Internet Empire, and they continue to encourage others to build their dreams and reach for the stars. Thanks also to Darren Stephens, his wife Jackie and his assistant Jo Munro, who give of their time and their knowledge with ease and generosity of spirit. I have also found along the way that people just seem to go out of their way to help me and you will find a long list of "thank you's" at the front of the book. There is a very good reason for this: without the assistance and kindness of the people who touch my life, I would not have got this far – their faith and belief in me propels me forward and, in my doing so, hopefully I can do the same for others.

We can all be inspired by the great politicians, sports people, actors, the volunteers, the mums and dads who live in our street, who achieve their goals and yet are compelled to do more and to help others live a life that is just a little bigger, a little brighter and a little more whole. So strap yourself in and – no matter your faith, your thoughts on religion, on God, on creation – have a read and maybe, just maybe, try one or two things, add to things that you may be already doing. See what happens and keep your mind and your heart open. Miracles really do happen.

Right about now you may be thinking: "So what are the 7 steps?" Well for starters, to make them really easy to remember, they just happen to spell MIRACLE. If we follow them in no particular order, we find many miracles and our spirit or our soul. Let me hasten to add I speak from my experience in writing this book and I am sure that people will have different experiences and I look forward to hearing from any of you about your beliefs and experiences. This book is not meant to replace anything you already believe in; rather it is an explanation that may make things seem a little easier to understand. It may also help you to build on practices that you may already be developing, and that is the beauty of it. Your belief is your belief and I am not trying to change it. I may challenge your thinking and I am sure that you will know what I mean as we continue.

Once you start to recognize those events in your life as miracles and step into the slipstream, even within the slipstream you can find yourself challenged. That challenge can sometimes strike you at odd and unexpected times. I have been challenged greatly in trying to write this book. The latest challenge involved my mother. She is now 84 and still active and happily living in her own home. We had been out to celebrate my birthday and Mum had driven herself home. She had a sore knee and was a bit slower than usual in walking from the garage, which has an automatic closing door. As she passed under the door, it knocked her to the ground and afterwards she found that she could not get back up. She spent that rainy and windy night on the garage floor. Luckily I found her 12 hours later. The paramedics were amazed at her condition; Mum herself described her survival as a Miracle. I see that divine spark within my mother that gave her the wherewithal to pull cardboard around her head to lock out the wind, to place a polystyrene lid on her legs and to put her feet in the box. All these things allowed her to maintain a good body temperature and increased her chance of survival. That's just a hint of some of the wonderful stories that you will share in reading this book, and the first of some of the miraculous things

Introduction

that happen to ordinary people that make extraordinary stories. For me, I like to think there is a little bit of Richard Branson in all of us. He seems to epitomize the use of the slipstream, both in his planes and his life. Imagine if we all harnessed that energy together. What endless adventures and possibilities of hope, love and understanding could be forged?

> "The jet stream is a very strong force and pushing a balloon into it is like pushing up against a brick wall, but once we got into it, we found that, remarkably, the balloon went whatever speed the wind went."
>
> Sir Richard Branson

I have found my way to a wonderful group of people who really display the slipstream in action. Each member of the Hunter Coaching Network has their own business, but they work as a team to promote coaching to the wider audience. This team provides our local community with high quality services that as individuals, we would not be able to do, but as a collective we enhance, support and inspire. My thanks to every member of the network. www.huntercoaching.com.au

I also just want to personally thank you up front for buying this book and taking a chance on finding something in it that will help you or just interest you. Not only do you make me feel like I have contributed something to my time and place in the world, you are also helping others. Ten percent of the profits are to be shared between two Not-For-Profit organizations. Both have a special place in my heart for some very real reasons. The Better Life Foundation http://www.thebetterlifefoundation.net/ helps villages in South Pacific Nations organize themselves in order to educate themselves, create an income stream and become self sufficient. Check out their website and don't hesitate to donate more: I do when I can. The other organization is Orphan Angels and it looks at trying to encourage and support adoption. My husband and I are adopting ourselves and we know the difficulties faced in achieving this. Our greater despair comes from knowing that there are some children who might otherwise be legitimately adopted, who languish in orphanages throughout the world. Orphan Angels' Ambassador is Deborah Lee Furness, who is not only inspiring to watch as an actor or director, but also has a passionate and eloquent understanding of these issues. Let's hope that some kind of miracle happens and all children can be given greater rights in this world and the bright start that we all deserve. So check out the website and know that you are doing some good just by buying my book. You have already paid something and given not once but multiple times in one transaction – how cool is that? So thank you and let's get going.

> "The child must know that he is a miracle, that since the beginning of the world there hasn't been, and until the end of the world there will not be, another child like him.""
> Pablo Casals

M – Mastery of the Mystery

M – MASTERY OF THE MYSTERY

> "...the teaching of your own religion must be in your heart. That's very important. Only then will you have an experience of it that is of real value, otherwise it is simply a piece of knowledge in your head and when you are faced with problems in your life, it won't be of any help." - the Dalai Lama

Miraculous events have long held a fascination for many and people have tried to explain these events in terms of their current terms of reference. In bringing the recognition of miracles into our lives, one of the simplest and most profound things to do is locate that place of mindfulness. Mindfulness is a term that has seeped into our language from Eastern traditions and is closely connected to meditation. When we are mindful, we are in the present moment. We are in the here and now; nothing matters except what is in our understanding at that time. When we can truly stay in the moment, we begin to see how things work, how we do things in our daily life, how we interact and treat ourselves and others. We begin to lift the veil on our actions and see our true selves.

We can start listening to those things around us that have voice. There are truly wonderful things in nature constantly giving voice to make our day more full and yet less hectic. We can also tune into our own breathing and the miracle that finds our diaphragm going in and out automatically to drive our bodily system. We can even hear our own heart beat as we tune into an awareness of the now. We are able to find the miracle that is ourselves as we do this. When we find that moment of peace, that gap between the constant monkey thoughts that bombard us on a daily basis, then we begin to place those things that we want to think about in the gap. We begin to see the world as we wish to see it, we begin to see our connections at work and we begin to see miracles unfold.

Finding this state of mindfulness also brings us in line with our being. There are many ways to do this. Meditation is only one, yet very effective way. Prayer is another form that helps people to find the gap and find the peace in their lives and invite more and more peace to them. Contemplation in nature, just being immersed in the beautiful surroundings, allows a freeing of the day to day and a return to a quiet that you dream of. Yet we cannot always easily return to the daily whirlwind of our modern lives.

When we reach this mindful state, and practice to bring it into our lives more and more, we become more and more aware of the things that we want in our lives. We begin to focus on those things and, as we think more about them, we begin to see how they can manifest for us. Opportunities that once seemed in the distance start to open up. The romance that had died in a relationship rekindles, or that job that you really want suddenly becomes available, and you see your thoughts are also guiding your outcomes. It is sometimes difficult to acknowledge this and you might find that it is much easier to think, "Oh that's just a coincidence, or nothing to do with me," but acknowledge the wonder that you are and you begin to think, just maybe, that divine spark within you is reaching you half way and showing you a whole other world that you think is beyond your reach.

We start to reconnect to that memory that we are born with, that we are miraculous. Our very coming into being is a miracle. As children, we think that the world revolves around us. We act in this way and our desires are met and we draw to us those things and people that best meet our needs at the time. We have a wonder of all things large and small and we look to nature as a gift and spend inordinate amounts of time watching, listening, learning and playing in the playground of our world. As we grow older, we move away from this wondrous thinking and learn to limit and deny our connection to the whole fabulous divine matrix. We connect to new patterns of thought, which come to us from others who have learned them from others, who in turn have passed them down to meet the needs of society at the time. The joy in small things and childlike wonder disappears from us and we walk in the world as if we have something to remember, but we just don't have the time, the energy, the resources left to remember or find what that is.

In order to master ourselves and the mystery again we need to find that gap, that space in time, so we can regain our truth and walk with a wonder that does not diminish, even when we are challenged by the day to day complexities of our time on earth. It is when we are most challenged that our strength comes to find the freedom to keep going, to move beyond the problem, to work through to a solution, to know that everything is okay and will work out for the greater good: that we have everything we need to understand and face the day to day, in fact we have had it ever since we were born.

So why meditate or find a way to connect to that peace? It really can settle and calm even the most challenging moments of our day. The way you choose to do this is really down to personal choice. Daily seems to help me most, but for others their weekly visit to their church, synagogue, mosque, or whatever is their chosen place of worship, connects them back to this space. Finding the time to just breathe deeply and consciously; breathing like this three or four times day can also help to return us to a present state of mind and one that allows us to move through situations that may be troubling to us. Sometimes those situations which bring us the most joy also bring us the most challenge, to find that space which allows us to experience the moment fully. Some people reading this will think "none of that really sits for me, I just go down to the beach or the park and have lunch and find some time to myself". You know what? You are doing just what I am talking about. You are giving yourself that time in the day where you find the gap and move beyond the chaotic world that surrounds us.

It is when we take this time that we begin to realize and comprehend the universe's magnificence and our place in that realm. We find the quiet to connect ourselves to God in a way that sits with us and we connect to that space no matter what we choose to call it. For God, the universe, the Divine Matrix is not worried by the name: it is more interested in knowing that we have connected and are beginning to pay attention. We are finally giving reverence to ourselves and the fabulous link we provide to the whole. We are a part of the whole and we can see that it is truly remarkable.

We can make these discoveries on our own and for some really privileged individuals this is the way they have always lived their lives. They have never lost this awareness and they struggle to understand how we ever could. Others have learned from those who have experienced great wonders in their own lives and become the teachers for us to learn from and to question, to share our understandings and experiences and to grow in the process. For the teacher also learns from the student and this shared endeavour further adds to the wonder of the experience for both. So if you feel the need; find an elder in your church, join a group that sits with your ideals, visit the holy men of your beliefs or of other beliefs. Start to go to seminars that are regularly run by the people that I have mentioned earlier. Go to the websites of Beyond Success, Global One, Pat Mesiti – see what courses and offerings may be there. As you begin to look, things will start to resonate for you and you will discover new ideas.

As we begin to develop a practice that allows us a rest from the daily doings of our world, we begin to see how things come to us more easily. We also find that we might have more energy for doing some of those things that we easily put off, and we certainly find that our levels of patience begin to climb; especially patience for ourselves and our journey. Our learning is not always easy and we forget that we should first be kind to ourselves and love ourselves so that we can do this for all we meet and encounter.

When we do this, our mental attitude begins to hold us firmly in all aspects of our daily life. We also begin to feel our intuition a little more clearly and this guides us through the day and beyond with a greater ease. We do have intuition: we just forget to listen. We forget to listen to that integral part of us that wants the best for us and is constantly seeking to provide us with those things we are thinking about. Balancing our mental attitude allows this hidden aspect of ourselves to connect us to the greater whole and become part of the slipstream to bring things into our world. Thinking in positive terms is best; for we want to bring the best into our world, and bringing that into our hearts and minds is the starting place.

In finding this stillness on a daily basis we are also able to begin listening to our heart and find our major purpose in life. For in life we have a purpose and it may be big or small, it may be near or far, but it is there and when we begin to hear this song, we find clues popping up all over the place to guide us to achieving our divine goal. Along this path things can still seem mysterious and yet we seem to have an inbuilt switch that wants to find our hand and allow us to commune with God, our higher self and begin to bring that other world into our daily life. To ignite that divine spark and set forth on creating our best and most fabulous outcomes, dip into the slipstream daily and expect that it is our right to watch the miracles flow to us. Big and small, there are no limits, only those that we place through fear or grasping.

Once we begin to hear the music of our soul, we are uplifted and can see bliss in situations that once seemed to only contain a narrow field of view. We become conscious, as if for the first time, that there is more to this life on earth and that we have a wonderful playground in which to grow and move forward. We share a connection to each other that is not always immediately apparent and we can easily forget. If we just think of us having a universal purpose, then we are already connected; for in seeking to find God, we experience that mystery of the other world which seems veiled to us. As we do this, individually and collectively, we begin to hear the music of our heart and move closer, ever closer, to our soul.

So we begin to manifest things in our lives and our attention to them, our attitude towards them, our attitude to ourselves and to others brings forth the slipstream and allows us to contemplate further on who we really are - and so we see how to begin the mastery of the mystery.

Action Steps:

1. Try learning to meditate, begin to pray
2. Go to your place of worship
3. Acknowledge nature and its beauty
4. Acknowledge your divine spark
5. Enrol in a course that's new
6. Practice breathing consciously 4 or 5 times a day

> "Mindfulness Is The Miracle By Which We Master And Restore Ourselves. Consider, For Example: A Magician Who Cuts His Body Into Many Parts And Places Each Part In A Different Region--Hands In The South, Arms In The East, Legs In The North, And Then By Some Miraculous Power Lets Forth A Cry Which Reassembles Whole Every Part Of His Body. Mindfulness Is Like That--It Is The Miracle Which Can Call Back In A Flash Our Dispersed Mind And Restore It To Wholeness So That We Can Live Each Minute Of Life."
>
> Thich Nhat Hanh, "Miracle of Mindfulness"

M – Mastery of the Mystery

Paul Blackburn's Thoughts on Miracles

PAUL BLACKBURN'S THOUGHTS ON MIRACLES

We talk about expecting to see miracles all the time. The meaning of the word miracle is the unusual, the unexpected, the impossible, the thing greater than could have happened via our own personal resources or power. In some of our workshops we say people should expect a miracle, that's the very minimum you should expect simply because we expect to see that. Now what we mean by that is some healing. If you use the classic biblical description, Jesus healed somebody, a leper, or whatever. What we see in our workshops is people can get over something that's been bothering them for 20 or 30 years. They can get over it in half an hour, so to us, miracle is probably an easy word to use but also an accurate one. We expect to see miracles turn up regularly each day. The great thing about miracles, or maybe the not so great thing about miracles, is they're unpredictable so you don't know how far away the next one is. It could be a couple of seconds away or it could be several hours or a day or two. In ordinary life, we'd be pretty impressed if we got a miracle a week and, because of the industry that we work in, we expect to see them much more regularly than that.

We acknowledge the fact that it's wonderful, that it's spontaneous, that what's happened is something that we weren't expecting to have happen. The jury's still out for me on where miracles come from. I understand that everybody has their own version and their own opinion, and I respect that. My personal version is that I was brought up as a Christian, although I don't call myself a Christian now, and I like to live by the 10 commandments, but I don't go to church and I don't pray to a God called Jesus. I like the Buddhist idea of "God is who you think God is", and at the very minimum there is a thing there called the universe. We can refer to a power greater than ourselves, that if there is such a being, then we're as much a part of that being as it is of us, and to separate us from this higher being is a hard thing. If that being exists and we must be a part of it, therefore, the expression "I am God" is valid for me, not that I think I walk on water.

The Dalai Lama says "Stick with your God," so I like that idea. To people whose God is Islamic in nature I say well good on you, I wouldn't want to change you from that. To people whose God is Christian in nature, I wouldn't want to change you from that. I don't subscribe to the "There can only be one version or one religion." Underneath it all, they're all a bit the same and this character called God is a bit above these differentiated versions that come out in the form of either Christianity or Islam.

I really didn't expect miracles. There were all the biblical examples of miracles but there weren't miracles described in our day to day life when I was a kid; in the beginning of my life they were all remote and certainly past tense. I spent 20 years in the wilderness when I left high school and went to find my way forward in life by getting a job and those sort of things. As I was brought up to be an average person in an average world with an average pay cheque I thought I wasn't going to see any miracles and I wasn't going to create any either. Once I got into the personal development industry, I noticed that miracles could occur on a regular basis, and they did, and it was everybody's right to expect a miracle, and that in fact, they ought to be a part of your life. In fact, I remember reading a quite complex book at the time called "A Course in Miracles" when it first came out. That was the first time that I ever entertained the idea that you could do a course on how to produce miracles. It was revolutionary to me, and now I just expect them.

This book was a turning point for my mother. My mother had always wanted to be a Christian. She was 1 of 2 daughters to a very strict Church of England couple, my grandparents, and her sister, my Aunty Joan, took religion seriously and went to live in a farming community where they were very devout and the major thing in life was to be poor and to be spiritual. I remember my mother saying to me that she wished she could get a faith; she said "I just can't make myself believe." When "A Course in Miracles" came out, she latched onto that and it was a turning point for her. For me it was just a bunch of exercises that I could undertake that would enhance my spirituality, without kicking me into a designated church or religion, even though the people that wrote the book turned out to be Christian. For me, it was one more tool along the way, it was a personal change, not by a revolution, but by a series of one degree changes. I've often heard it said that if you drive a boat out of Sydney Harbour heading directly east and you change course by one degree every hour, then your boat will hit Australia because it will do a complete U-turn and you won't notice the thing happening because it's only one degree every hour and, as soon as you're out of sight of land, you can't tell which way you're facing. Anyway, that was pretty much it for me, a series of one degree turns added up to ten percent, and then it added up to 20 and away you go. So, the catalyst along the way, "A Course in Miracles" was one of the degrees that added up to such change.

It was an accumulation of slight changes triggered by dissatisfaction. So I began thinking there had to be more to life and there had to be some reason why things were the way they were, and surely I could achieve more than I was. So dissatisfaction, brought about by a business failure, brought that into sharper focus. I read a personal development book or two and then I read one that made a lot of sense. I went and did a personal development course which was along the lines of the book that made sense, and I thought "ok, that's it, these people have got it figured out". So the final turn was a big one I guess, it was probably 40% or 50% of the turnaround and it was around that book and course, in 1982 I think.

I was prompted to do the work we do by a number of things. One of the things that happened was that the course, well, nowadays that course wouldn't be so exciting because a lot of the material is now common knowledge, but 27 years ago it was pretty revolutionary. I thought, "I need to be around this material otherwise it'll just be a flash in the pan, it'll go". So in thinking about how I could remain in contact with the people who ran the course, what became obvious to me was that what I was missing was being a school teacher; but I didn't want to go back to teach kids. I wasn't missing being a school teacher, I was missing being a teacher; and the idea that I could teach these things that I just learned to other adults was very appealing. Not just because of the material, but because of the concept of teaching and how I'd always enjoyed it.

It was a perfect marriage: the ability to get back into teaching, which I'd been out of for a number of years, and the ability to teach adults who I prefer to teach than kids. So couple that with material that I was personally on fire about and there was really no turning back, and I've been involved with it ever since. I actually worked with a corporation that taught that course for a couple of years and then we both went our separate ways, quite amicably, and Mary and I have been running the business called Beyond Success for 25 years now. I said in the beginning that it was a big turning point. It was big, but I have trouble when it comes to "what is my greatest miracle", because what happens is that what we see as a miracle today is pretty ordinary tomorrow. The greatest miracle that I've ever experienced is the birth of our two children. How could that happen if it wasn't for the miracle of meeting and marrying Mary, and how could that happen if it wasn't for the miracle of being a school teacher and appointed to the same school in which she was already a teacher.

So miracles cascade, or to put it another way, these turning points add up. If you keep taking left hand turns they add up and you go in circles. So what is my greatest miracle? It's the relationship between Mary and me and the difference that she's made in my life, the different man that I am because of her influence over me. The change in me, that's nothing short of miraculous, not that she brought it about, but that she instigated it. I made those changes, but Mary was the trigger so to speak, and then along came the kids.

I think our business is a miracle itself. Really, any business that stays in existence for more than a few years, actually survives and ends up making money is probably a miracle when you look at the number of failures. You look at the business and say, "What a miracle that I get to work in a field that I absolutely love, with people that I adore, with material that I'm entranced by." In my mind, that is a collection of miracles, but the whole thing itself is a miracle, to be able to run a business and determine how that business goes and be allowed to play with it and work with it, it's all miraculous.

I remember the day I stopped smoking, 13 years ago now, and at the time that was a miracle because I hadn't been able to do it before, literally impossible to do before: there's a miracle. I don't even think about that now, it's just one of those things. I could not pick up a cigarette now and deliberately smoke it. I couldn't by accident, I doubt if you could get me to do it by hypnosis, that's a miracle. I haven't thought about that achievement for weeks and weeks and weeks, even months. So that's perhaps one of the sad things about miracles, that we tend to not continue to acknowledge that they are miracles.

Paul Blackburn's Thoughts on Miracles

We want more in our life and that is why we become blasé about miracles. Your next house is supposed to be bigger and better than your current house and your next car is supposed to be better than the last one and all those sort of things. As human beings, we're always wanting more and so a lot of things that are delivered to us via a miracle we go "yep, you beauty, next." The basic component to my current level of good health is the fact that I no longer smoke. So what was miraculous before is now bedrock, it's just bottom line. So it has become ordinary because: (a) we want more; and (b) many miracles allow the next thing to happen. So the miracle of our children being born is fantastic, now we have to work on the miracle of a wonderful relationship with them. So we tend to work on the relationship with them, and that takes a bit of focus away from the amazement about the fact that they exist, that they come from us, the whole miraculous aspect of it.

We tend not to acknowledge these spectacular things. We fall into this trap of wanting more, and thinking that more is better and fail to have an attitude of gratitude. There's not too many people who, when they get up each day, say "Righto, well what I better do is I better give thanks for the fact that I woke up instead of dying in my sleep, I better give thanks for the fact that there's plenty of air, there's plenty of water, there's plenty of food, I live in a free country and there's no bullets flying around." We get up and we get busy and we rush around the day, wondering if we're going to get to work on time, and getting to work on time is just not so miraculous really.

The attitude of gratitude is critically important, for several reasons, but the first and most obvious reason is that it's only an attitude of gratitude that's going to allow you to move on. If you're not grateful for what you've got, then why would any more turn up? It is fundamental. Even if you're having yourself on and you're making it all up, you have a much better day if you're grateful than if you're not. It actually goes to mindset. We all know somebody who's going to be miserable tomorrow and they've made their decision already and that's because they're not grateful about how things are at the moment, they're not filled with joy about being alive. They've just forgotten to acknowledge how good it is, as it is.

Six years ago, the doctors told me I had three years to live. So I'm three years past that so-called deadline, which is something I'm very grateful about. So there's another miracle, was that my greatest miracle? There are probably thousands of them, but there's one that I didn't think of first and that is the fact that I'm alive today. Everybody copes differently with being told you've got three years to live. I've met people who cope very badly with it, and those who cope very well, and everybody in between. It's an intensely personal thing in terms of how you cope with it, and what you do about it, and that has a lot to do with emotional intelligence, which is your ability to use your thinking to affect your feeling. So the way that I tackled it was to first of all find out what the medical profession thought could be done. They said okay, we can give you an operation and then there could be radiotherapy and then there could be chemotherapy, this that and the other with various levels of what they thought it might do, and you know, without saying it, how it might extend my life, or not, and how long they thought I might live.

Initially I did not cope very well. When the Doctor first gave me that scenario, I had actually gone to the Doctor's by myself and I left the Doctor's and I rang Mary and, as I was saying the words to her "I have cancer," I burst into tears. It wasn't until I actually said the words that it actually hit. And it hit pretty hard. It took a while for me to regain my composure enough to be able to look at it with clear eyes and develop some kind of strategy and get a sense of bringing my normal self into what was basically an attack on something. Eventually I went to war on it and put in a big effort as far as the recovery is concerned and things that I could do. The miracle was up the top of the list, a miracle was going to be just fine with me, so I put my order in for one and, luckily enough, got one.

I did things that I believed would help my recovery. I'm a big believer in meditation, and the reason that I'm a big believer in it is that I've seen it produce such spectacular results for so many people. Now that we've been in the business we're in, part of which is teaching meditation, for 25 years, we're talking about literally thousands of people that I've seen whose lives have been dramatically, massively, powerfully affected by them going and learning to meditate and then doing it on a regular basis. So that's what I went straight to. I thought "Meditation is going to be the way that I go with this." You know, like the plumber's tap's always dripping and the painter's house always needs a coat of paint, I wasn't actually really up to date with my meditation practices, so I found a renewed level of commitment.

Whether the Doctors had said to me, look you've got a very mild case and we've got an operation that's guaranteed to fix it, I think meditation is going to accelerate every kind of healing, so it was never going to be a question about that. I might have been a bit rusty, but many people will tell you that one of the gifts of cancer is that it slows you down, it makes you stop and think. During that time I realised that there was never going to be a time when I was not a great meditator, I was not going to get out of practice again, so for the rest of my life as long as that will be, and I plan for that to be very long, my meditation practice will be current and up to speed. And so far, that's the way it's been.

I work what most people would call pretty hard. I probably do

100 hours a week. The reason I say "probably" is that I don't count them, so I don't really know. The reason I can do those huge hours is because I love what I'm doing, so that's a miracle. But I back that up with action; you can't expect God to do it all by himself and if I were God I'd probably like to help those who are helping themselves, or showing some sign of getting involved in the process at least. I'm quite fit, I eat healthily, I'm a bit of a fanatic about food in terms of what I will and won't eat, so I'd rather go hungry than eat rubbish, so that's what I do.

I was brought up in a family of what we call bread-heads, those people who eat bread every time they see it and can't resist it. One of the complimentary practitioners that I went to, a naturopath, said to me that in 1927 this guy called Otto Walberg won the Nobel prize for proving that cancer thrives in a glucose rich environment, so what you need to do is go onto a grain-free diet that will drop the blood sugar level to the point where the cancer can't survive, and yet you'll be quite healthy. I've found that to be true. I can't remember the last piece of bread I ate, so I'm a bit fanatical like that. What I've noticed is that I don't miss it, like I don't miss cigarettes. In the beginning it seems terrible and the change is dramatic, but really, our taste adjusts, and so I'm fit, I'm healthy, I'm strong, I lift weights and I attend aerobic exercise. I don't lift weights like a maniac, I just do enough so that my body has to work and I think that that's my contribution to making sure that miracle doesn't get wasted. My belief is that the miracles will stop coming if you don't treat them nice.

It's along the lines of the attitude of gratitude really. Why would God, or the universe, or whichever expression you like to use, send you more if you're not grateful about what it has sent already? One of my ways of paying attention to my miraculous recovery is to work on my health and fitness. I am reinforcing my gratitude. I get bored doing exercise, but I'd rather be bored

Paul Blackburn's Thoughts on Miracles

than dead, so that's why I'm doing it. It's where my values are. It's obviously not going to get in front of my relationships and other things that are more important; like telling the truth and having integrity and those kinds of things, but it's going to be up there, it's certainly going to hit the top end. I think you've got to go with "the body is a temple". You can't maintain a healthy self image or self esteem if you're willing to poison yourself with too much alcohol, nicotine, bad practices, bad language or all those kinds of things. How you treat yourself is really important and that helps you to treat other people better. We can all achieve miracles and one of the great places to start is your own miracle. You yourself are a miracle, so if you are, then maybe you should act that way. Why would you not treat yourself like you're a miracle? If you're worried about paying the bills and you're cranky with the kids and all that sort of stuff, it's a bit hard to look at yourself as a miracle. You've actually got to pay attention to the fact that you are a miracle and the fact that you need to behave as if you are.

You remind yourself that you are a miracle when you treat those around you as if they are. It's one of those things where the Buddhists talk about mindfulness; placing great importance on simple things is the reminder that the very fact that you're breathing is a miracle, a whole miraculous process. Just breathing, that's a start. It's also something that I use as a start to the day. When I wake up of a morning, I go to the mirror and I breathe on it and it fogs up and I say "You beauty." I can start with being grateful about the fact that I'm breathing. As a friend of mine says, every day above the ground is a good one.

In our workshops, we are present to miracles for other people and it is humbling and inspiring. I feel very humble when I see how much any one individual is capable of. For most people, a miraculous recovery or healing or breakthrough comes as a direct result of their courage to get in and deal with the thing which has given them such a hard time for so long. I predominantly see miracles as a consequence of courage being displayed. I always find that inspiring and, when I'm inspired, I do more and I expect more of myself. I'm a much better person because I think inspiration allows you to seek, to do and to be more without wanting to have more power in the world or to be a bigger and better person. It's very difficult to put into words what it's like. I'm continually amazed when I see something happen that could not happen before. There's a gladness about how lucky I was to see it, so I end up feeling like the world's full of magnificent human beings and I'm just lucky enough to be around lots of them. I feel like my life is full of very high calibre, high quality, people and I can't describe that any other way except to say I feel lucky. There's a theory that says there's no such thing as luck, so I'm not too sure how I'm going to explain that.

There's still plenty of mystery around the whole thing. Even though I know what to do and how to conduct these workshops so that the miracles happen, there's still plenty of mystery around it. We have a bunch of procedures and attitudes and beliefs and that sort of stuff, but there's still plenty of mystery. Here's the funny thing. Mystery only exists until you find out what's behind it. A mystery, by its very nature, is something that we can't explain or aren't able to articulate. Then we get a breakthrough and we can explain it, so what used to be a mystery becomes known, and then it's not a mystery anymore. There's an element of yearning, there's an element of wanting to go further or wanting to know more.

The other thing that I see, which is like miracles, is that I don't think human beings can learn slowly. I've been a full-time professional teacher since 1973. That's a lot of years to watch hundreds of thousands of people in the learning process and

Paul Blackburn's Thoughts on Miracles

going through their own way of learning. The conclusion I've come to is that we can't learn slowly, we just suddenly get things. There's a time when 2 + 2 = 4 is a mystery or is hard for us to know about, and then all of a sudden, boom, it goes into our heads. Most people are familiar with studying for an exam by just going over and over and over and, when we reflect on it and ask "When did you begin to understand it?" they say "Well, I don't know it just all of a sudden went click." So along the line of the miracle thing is the nature of how we learn, so that taps into the whole miracle thing. Ask any brain scientist and they'll tell you the brain itself is a miracle. The fact that it can learn and continue to learn is yet another one.

There's a lot of evidence for the idea of cumulative knowledge, where each person takes it one step further than the last one, and you wouldn't have trouble maintaining the argument. We also have the blinding flash. Everyone reading this book will have an "uh huh" moment, where they suddenly understand something that they didn't before. We have those "uh huh" moments when things just go click, and sometimes we can't explain why they go click, they just do, and those moments are also probably in the miracle category. I have had some of those "uh huh" moments during the 25 odd years that I've been doing the Beyond Success personal development side of things.

They're a pretty common occurrence, but quite often they will happen when I'm explaining something to somebody else. I'll be teaching something and as I'm teaching it, I suddenly get a sense of an insight into it that I have not perceived before. That's the thing that keeps me doing it. It's fantastic and it's a wonderful thing to see other people having breakthroughs, but if you weren't having them yourself then you'd be a spectator. I think everybody who's been a spectator at something would like to have a go at it, be it tennis or whatever. One of the most startling revelations in my entire life has been the fact that I am my own source of wisdom and that everybody is, and having that experience is quite extraordinary. To be teaching something that I've been teaching for 20 years and then suddenly understand another level to it, in the middle of explaining it to someone else, is another form of miracle. The wisdom comes from within, but it's also without, from that greater being, call it God or the universe, that wisdom is within us, but also part of the whole.

I've had that experience of it not coming from me. I can recall numerous situations where I was confronted with a situation where there was no possibility that I would have an answer or a solution, and yet when I opened my mouth there it was. The answer was transformational for the person that I said it to and yet I don't know where it came from. I think the temptation there is to say "Well, it didn't feel like it came from me, so it came from…" and that's where you put your preference, that it came from God, the universe or whatever. In ancient times, the Egyptians would say, "Okay, when I said that there was a cat in the room, so therefore it came from the cat." They link the cat in and then that's what happens. We give responsibility to that which we are predisposed to give it to. A Christian's going to say it came from God, but an atheist is going to say it came from within you. I'm much fonder of the idea we started with in the beginning of the chapter: that is if there is a God, then I must be part of that and therefore, to a certain extent, I am God. So it came from within me, but God is within me, so it all gets like the chicken and the egg.

"Where there is great love, there are always miracles."
Willa Sibert Cather (1873-1947)

Paul Blackburn's Thoughts on Miracles

I - Invite the Infinite Intelligence of Our Invisible Soul

I – INVITE THE INFINITE INTELLIGENCE OF OUR INVISIBLE SOUL

> *"I know this world is ruled by infinite intelligence. Everything that surrounds us - everything that exists—proves that there are infinite laws behind it. There can be no denying this fact. It is mathematical in its precision." - Thomas Edison (1847-1931)*

Finding inspiration in our lives can sometimes be difficult. If we allow the daily routine, the problems, the issues, the disasters to mount, then we often forget to look at and give thanks for the things that are truly wonderful and that do bring about joy in our lives. As I am writing this, I'm cruising through the Bermuda Triangle aboard a beautiful ship called the Independence of the Seas. The sun is dancing on the water and reflecting the beauty of nature to all who take the time to look. As a small child growing up in suburban Australia, I was always fascinated with the mystery of the Marie Celeste, a boat that was found floating soulless in these same waters. A sense of awe descends on me that, so many years later, here I am aboard a state of the art ship in these waters. Never in my imagination did I ever think I would be sailing those same waters. However, consider for just a second, that the boat on which I am sailing was probably never dreamed of until one or more heads got together and designed the ultimate (at least for the time being) cruise ship. For when we invite that divine spark in us to fire up, then we really are only limited by our imaginations.

I – Invite the Infinite Intelligence of Our Invisible Soul

Rejoicing in nature or in the achievements of our fellow man really brings us closer to that infinite intelligence that is given many names and that I have referred to as God. For when we seek God, then we might find him in each and every one of us, in all the things we can perceive and are yet to perceive. We truly begin to see what a wonderful playground we are given on earth and how we can rejoice in our place here and make this world everything that we want. For one of the great outcomes of spending the time each day, or as often as you can, in contemplation or meditation, is that strengthening of the connection that you have with the other – with God.

God is in all things, but how can that be? If the divine spark is within everything and everyone, then God is there waiting for us to seek, to listen, to see, to ask. We are a moment away from a connection – like a light switch on the wall. Turning the switch on costs nothing and can only enrich our lives. Really, if that switch is waiting there for all of us, isn't that a great miracle that we each already have? Our lives truly are programmed to find a way to connect to that peace. The choice to do so is ours. How we do so is also something that many people wonder about. If we could break down the barriers of religion, ethnicity, sexuality, intellect, class and all those things that we nominate as being hurdles, if we just trust in our spirit to guide us, then where would we be in this world? I would like to think that we would be ever closer to God and to all the wonders that we dreamt about as children. That we would be approaching a plane where unconditional love is all there is.

Just for a second imagine that world, what would it be like, how would it function, how would you feel, what could you achieve with limitless abundance? It's hard to do in our times, when we are faced each night with the news of our local areas and the wider world. The news leaves the impression that we can never achieve this nirvana on earth. Remember though, God is limitless, ageless and timeless, and what if enough of us wanted to find this for our world? Infinite intelligence may just meet us to find that unique world and leave an enduring legacy of harmony. As individuals, we can bring those changes into our world and bring about the slipstream and, just maybe, turn the tide.

We each hold a key within us that unlocks the connection with God. Accessing that key from within is really the secret to the success of your connection. No matter what you participate in through your church, your bible study, your prayer meetings, through coaching, through commune with nature, the external is merely the vehicle for you to find the internal connecting point. In the point of connection, divine grace touches your heart, body, and mind. You are forever changed in the process, but that change does not mean that you do not exist in the daily and wider world, it is rather the daily and wider world doesn't always have the same impact.

One of the simplest ways to connect is to find that childlike wonder in the things around you. I am still amazed to be living on a small floating city just for a brief moment in time. Like a child, I wonder at how they can feed nearly 6,000 people 24 hours a day, how they can navigate serenely through swells and storms and what imagination brought this man-made wonder to life; for it is our imagination that can create the world of our desires. Even now I chuckle when I see the latest video watch – which looks like it comes straight from a Dick Tracy cartoon. I wonder if the man who imagined Dick Tracy and that watch had any idea that in a time of the future that watch would be a reality. Walt Disney had a wonderful imagination and now so many children around the world can benefit from his vision, his belief and his childlike imagination - together they brought us

I – Invite the Infinite Intelligence of Our Invisible Soul

Adventureland, Fantasyland, Tomorrowland and Frontierland. If we could all suspend our disbelief and have the courage of our visions, our faith and our connection, what would you design for your life and a contribution to our world?

> *"If you can dream it, you can do it. Always remember that this whole thing was started with a dream and a mouse."* - Walt Disney

For we all have the potential to dream like Walt Disney, to break the 4 minute mile like Roger Bannister, even though it was said it couldn't be done by any human. We could all choose to work with children in third world countries and build schools and help communities to grow and be self sufficient. Our individual successes are only limited by our imaginations. Start to write down how you see your perfect world, write everything, draw a picture in words, draw a picture and find those things that make up your perfect world. Start a dream board and begin to visualize those things in your life. Your life is unique and your choices in life are relevant to you. They have an impact on us all, but they are choices for you alone. You may share a path with many or few through your choices, but make good ones and your potential success is unlimited.

In his books, Napoleon Hill talks about us being the Captain of our Souls. The greatest inventor of your success is you. The you that is one with the divine, the you that is connected to all others and to your higher self. You may find the seas rocky at times and, no doubt like us all, can make mistakes. Mistakes only provide a slight detour and then you can return to navigate your way, to take your higher guide and return to the slipstream of smooth waters, knowing that you always have the potential to achieve your goals; to invite those miracles into your life. A wise woman (thanks Deb) said to me once or twice, because I tend to be a slow learner, "Never, never, never give up." I seem to recall she turned blue at one point. I finally listened and then set my course back to my original plan. The words she used came from Winston Churchill and although he takes his place on the world stage because of his contribution during the World Wars and on the world stage, as an individual he was plagued with depression or the "Black Dog", as he called it. As human beings, we can have illness in our mind, body and hearts, but being able to connect with our spirit, our invisible soul, allows us to deal with whatever way this manifests and to comprehend ways around it.

The infinite intelligence also provides us with the initiative to do something with our lives. Whatever that something is, at some level it creates a ripple that brings about change. We don't always see that change but it can have reactions and responses that lead others to do something, to enter that slipstream and begin to create the life of their design. As we see others do this, then we begin to wonder how. We may even seek training and guidance from them and usually those people who have worked to find that direction are happy to help you on your way. Throughout civilization we have seen great achievements, and our times are no different, and we are still trying to find the way to complete our own lives on this planet. Take the initiative in your life and not only will your own life change but, like those ripples of so many before us, we can inspire the future.

So entering the slipstream and bringing miracles into our lives comes through us asking, through us actually acknowledging that we have a connection with something more than just our day to day. As we begin to acknowledge those small and great changes that may come about because of this request, we also

I – Invite the Infinite Intelligence of Our Invisible Soul

begin to see more and more come to us. We see that our belief in things being possible actually creates streams to bring them into our lives. Sometimes the challenge is to have persistence and perseverance and remember: "Never, never, never give up".

As we begin to ask and acknowledge, we may also notice that our intuition is actually giving us little hints along the way. Now that interpretation is really for the individual, but sometimes you think I don't want to do that, or go here and yet you do. Things seem to go pear-shaped and you remember that you really didn't want to be there or do that anyway. That is your intuition just reminding you. Once you start to recognize this more and more, and feel the difference, you can begin to rely on it. Your intuition is leading you through truth and to your true sense. That oneness allows us to begin to see how we function and how we can bring about change in our world and the ripples this creates.

The strength of our connection is really only hindered by the intensity with which we approach our desires. Putting our full feeling into what we want to achieve adds to the reality of it coming into our life. That slipstream operates in a way that still truly gives us the mystery and wonder that miracles are. They are not predictable, but they are certainly attainable. Like all things, as we acknowledge them, they come to us more and more. But they really are a way that the infinite intelligence can communicate with us. You can switch on that divine spark and have communion with God, whatever form that may take for you, and life just gets a whole lot brighter and leads you beyond the limits you may have previously set for yourself.

Littlewood's Law basically tells us that miracles really are inevitable. Littlewood defines a miracle as an exceptional event of special significance occurring at a frequency of one in a million. He assumes that during the hours in which a human is awake and alert, a human will experience one event per second, which may either be exceptional or unexceptional (for instance, seeing the computer screen, the keyboard, the mouse, the article, etc.). Additionally, Littlewood supposes that a human is alert for about eight hours per day.

As a result, under these suppositions, a human will have experienced 1,008,000 events in 35 days. Accepting this definition of a miracle, one can be expected to observe one miraculous occurrence within the passing of every 35 consecutive days – and therefore, according to this reasoning, seemingly miraculous events are actually commonplace. - Wikipedia

There is a probability of something miraculous occurring. It is interesting to see that mathematicians are even interested to look at miracles and their probability. They may argue that, because of Littlewood's Law, there is no such thing as a miracle. Yet the miracle of a mathematician's brain is truly wonderful; they can develop the formulas to take man to space to investigate the trajectory of planets and other celestial objects. Look at the legacy that Pythagoras left us with – yet, he was an ordinary man who dared to think outside the constraints of his times and his world.

Einstein is perhaps one of the greatest thinkers of recent times. He was an amazing thinker who had an intention to create new ideas and to think outside the square. He was also very sure that there was another that was meeting him in this process. He is often quoted and his example shows what we can achieve, when we create a world that we want to see, and that anything is possible. If we change our belief that we are limited, and instead believe that we have endless potential, then we have already begun to switch on our divine spark and launch ourselves into the slipstream of endless possibility. Allowing the wonder of this world to engulf us, and trusting in the outcomes of our desires, plays those miracles into our lives.

We invoke the spirit of our own divine nature and, as we believe, we see how things are possible. We can address those things that we want to achieve and suddenly, how something comes into our life doesn't really matter, we just accept that it can and it usually does. Ask in whatever way you find comfortable and those prayers are answered in wondrous ways.

Action plan:

1. Create a Dream board.

2. Focus on what you really want and maintain contact with the infinite intelligence.

3. Put feeling into your desired outcomes and remember that you are only limited by your own imagination.

4. Persevere in adversity, ask others for help in trying times.

> *"I am enough of an artist to draw freely upon my imagination. Imagination is more important than knowledge. Knowledge is limited. Imagination encircles the world." - Albert Einstein.*

Pat Mesiti's Thoughts on Miracles

PAT MESITI'S THOUGHTS ON MIRACLES

A miracle is a term to me. To me, a miracle is a supernatural experience and it's something that cannot really be explained in a natural sense. It's something that cannot be explained in a completely rational sense. I believe miracles come from God. I believe that God supernaturally intervenes in the lives of men and I believe it happens to believers and non-believers. I think sometimes we forget the supernatural element to what is often a very natural thing. For example, you and I breathe every day. Who gave us that? Where did that come from? I've just had a grandson born. The gift of life. How do I explain the soul that's in this little boy and in each and every one of us - it's something that's supernatural and you really can't put it into words. I believe that comes from God. As a Christian, that's my frame of reference for miracles.

Well, without wanting to sound weird, I've actually been in meetings with a little blind boy and his eyes opened. I've seen deaf people receive their hearing. I had an instance one day when I laid hands on a young man and a broken leg was completely healed. I've seen situations where people have had their prayers received and their cancer has been healed. Totally unexplainable. I do believe we underestimate the power of prayer in our lives. They've done surveys and discovered that those people that pray in times of distress find comfort and healing. I believe in the laying on of hands and prayer. Jesus said "lay your hands on the sick and they shall recover." He didn't say they may. He said they shall. Sometimes they do. Sometimes they don't. I can't explain it. I just know that I've seen literal miracles in my life and over the course of years, I've seen both the dark side of the supernatural and I've seen the God side of the supernatural.

Pat Mesiti's Thoughts on Miracles

The greatest miracle I have ever seen has been in hundreds and thousands of lives; it is the power of forgiveness for their sins. I've seen hardened criminals change. I've seen average mum's and dad's lives change. There is no substitute for what I believe is the new birth that comes through Jesus Christ. I've seen the miraculous change of addicts to totally, completely, different men and women. I've seen it affect the most hardened criminals; they melt to the power of forgiveness and the power of a new birth. You can't explain that either. We always talk about birthing in new age terms, but Jesus brings about a new birth. A new birth, where the old person is gone. He doesn't exist anymore and this new identity comes in, which is a God identity, and that's the greatest miracle I think I've ever seen. Even greater than seeing a little boy's eyes open or a deaf person's ears unblocked; that miracle of a life that cannot be explained outside of a divine epiphany, if you want to call it that. That's the greatest miracle I've ever seen.

Belief is sometimes needed for a miracle. Faith is an important part. One guy once said "Jesus, I believe but just help my unbelief". What an amazing statement of surrender to God. I believe he'll heal my unbelief. Help me grow.

When people experience a miracle, there is something special about it. You know this person was once blind and now they see. I mean, you get a sense that they have a peace about them. What is different about them? I have people tell me all the time "You're very different, Pat. You're a very different person." I go "You know well, keep asking the questions and I'll give answers." I try not to preach to people, but I think that when you're around a miracle, you sense it. Whether it be a pivotal miracle or an internal miracle, it's something you can't explain, you can only feel. At the end of the day, if you're a doubter and a sceptic, you're not going to feel anything, because where you stand is going to determine what you see. Have an open heart. I remember a friend of mine said "Can you see this?" and the guy said "No". My friend said, "Well, you can't see nothing when you close your eyes". Just open your eyes and your heart. Miracles are seen through the eyes of our hearts, not our physical eyes. The soul thinks in pictures. The heart sees in visions and dreams. Miracles can only really be seen through the heart. I don't know if that makes sense to you.

I think it's a yes and a no as to whether we can bring miracles into our lives. I think that yes, we can make miracles happen sometimes and other times, no, we can't. Sometimes, it's simply a response of faith where you just believe. The power of your will can sometimes intervene. People's cancers drop off and they're not even people of faith. It's the willpower. I mean, Lance Armstrong is a prime example. Other times it's a simple surrender to God. It's just like God chooses. How do we understand the mysteries of God? How do you understand infinite being with all knowledge and all power? How does a finite mind try to explain it? You can't. The limited can never explain the unlimited. The limited knowledge can never explain the all-knowledge of God. People say "Why did God let this happen?" I don't know. I'm not God. "Why didn't God do this?" I don't know. "Why did he do it for them and not for them?" I don't know the answer to that question. If I knew the answer to that question, I probably would be God. I think God reserves some things for himself. There are some things that this side of eternity will never have an answer to. So that's why I said yes and no as to whether we can bring miracles into our lives.

In some tales in the Bible, Jesus does miracles everywhere. Others say Jesus could do no miracles. Why was that? I don't know.

It's part of the great mystery. How do you explain air? I don't

Pat Mesiti's Thoughts on Miracles

know. I mean, you can explain it, but it still doesn't make sense that I breathe. How do I explain that I've got this alive body and then my soul leaves me and I'm just a shell? A shell that doesn't even look like me anymore? I can't explain it.

Forgiveness and the power of prayer are important for our connection to miracles, as is trust. Trust God. Trust in the person of Jesus Christ. I remember one day when I was in the Philippines and I was a minister at the time. There was a big riot going on and shotguns were going off everywhere and I was pretty freaked out. I remember God spoke to my heart. I said "God, I'm really scared" and he said "Do you trust me with your life?" And I said "Yes". He said "Then why don't you trust me with your death?" I think trust is a big thing. I think trust is very important just for the simple fact that you believe and hang on to that belief, in spite of what other people say. That's important. You'll always have the doubting Thomases around.

My friend Morris Goodman - who is the Miracle Man – has an incredible story. The doctors told him he'd never walk, never again. He said to his doctor "I'll walk out of here in six months and shake your hand." I asked him one day, what he thought of what the doctors said. He replied "It didn't matter what they said, it mattered what I said and what I felt". That was a pretty good answer. I think believing is important - if you don't know what God has said in his book, the Bible, you don't know what he can do. It would be really helpful if people just understood what God said and saw what he did - like the miracle of healing, the miracle of forgiveness.

Knowing that if I said "Geraldine, I'm going to pick up the phone at ten o'clock," you can trust the word that I'm going to do it, you know? That is what it is like when we trust God and allow him to bring miracles of healing and forgiveness into our lives. God loves to be trusted. God is pleased when he's trusted. He grieves when he's doubted. God's whole premise of creating man was to commune with man, to walk with man and to have man trust him. That makes God happy. I think it engenders miracles.

Just being around Morris, and other people like him, you sit back in amazement and you go, "How did this happen? You should be dead." I've got a mate of mine who was dying, absolutely dying, of cancer. We're talking skin and bone and then he's healed. His name is Brian. He's a minister. I can't explain it. I can't. Being around him, I say to him I remember when he was all but dead and now he lives again.

About a year ago, I had a guy pull me out at a meeting, where I was speaking, and he said, "I remember you. You're the guy who was that gangster when I was a kid at school and you did this and you did this and you did this". I said "Yeah, I'm pretty ashamed of that." and he goes, "I'm sitting there and thinking, I can't believe he's the same person". I went well, "That's the power of what God can do in a man's life". Being around heavenly experiences is an awesome thing.

> "Humanity is never so beautiful as when praying for forgiveness, or else forgiving another." Jean Paul

Pat Mesiti's Thoughts on Miracles

R - Recognise Results and Mould Your Reality

R – RECOGNISE RESULTS AND MOULD YOUR REALITY

> *"Hope is the companion of power, and mother of success; for who so hopes strongly has within him the gift of miracles."* - Jean Paul

In the last chapter, we spoke of the importance of never ever giving up. It is this resilience that is truly important to us in our lives. If we fail, as we sometimes will, is that a sign that we should stop? For some, that is enough to tell them to move on, to leave their job, their relationship, their country and try again, or stay and try again. For others, it is seen as a sign that they should give up on life, on hope of their divine spark and just leave this life. The tragedy for those people is that if they tried one more time, gave themselves that last chance, then they just may have found that the last chance was there waiting for them. For life has a way of giving us detours and challenges, but it is the way that we handle them that can make a huge difference in our lives and the lives of others.

On my most recent holiday, that was to become a personal odyssey of sorts for me, we decided to visit the Kennedy Space Center. As a child, I remember watching in awe as Man walked on the moon. I still recall watching the news reports of this momentous occasion. For years I kept a medal that commemorated these first tiny steps. Walking through the

R – Recognise Results and Mould Your Reality

Space Center my heart raced as I looked at different capsules, spacesuits and items commemorating Man's achievements with space travel. Years later, I also recalled the night that I was watching the crew of the Challenger space shuttle prepare for launch. I watched the faces board the shuttle. I had heard the enthusiasm of Christa McAuliffe, the first school teacher to be part of the crew.

> "I touch the future, I teach. I really appreciate that sentiment, that's going with me" – Christa McAuliffe

I watched in horror as the shuttle disintegrated shortly after takeoff. With all its checks and balances, NASA suffered a catastrophe of seemingly irreconcilable proportions, yet this did not stop the dream continuing. This negative outcome produced the resilience to never give up, to honour those lost lives by regrouping, recreating, reinventing and returning for a positive outcome for the future. That lives were lost is tragic, but their memory continues to inspire and drive man to greater heights in space travel. Their memory is etched over the skies of the Space Center, their legacy a reminder that failures happen, but the wonder of achievement surrounds us and inspires such potential to all those would be astronauts, both big and small.

We can use NASA as an example of recognising results and accepting our past mistakes. When we do this, we can improve our future outcomes and actually take the time to give thanks for all those times when things worked for us, for all the beautiful things that surround us, for the wonderful people who fill our lives and for the remarkable being that we each are. We begin to see that our life is filled with abundance and that we have a tap of sorts, that allows us to increase the flow and bring more into our lives. This continuing attitude of gratitude brings abundance ever closer to us and creates the world around us.

Our reaction to things in our lives is really important. The more was can find the gap between stimulus and response and take the time to acknowledge what is happening without reacting, the more we have space to choose our reaction. Instead of being driven by the outside events that can affect us, we can have a choice in deciding if they will affect us. NASA had a choice after the Challenger disaster. They had a gap in their shuttle programme, but they never gave up their dreams, their goals and their visions for space travel. Whilst the gap in this case is not the gap that I am talking about, it does illustrate that we are able to choose how we react to things and how we follow on from the disasters that can befall our day. We have the opportunity to check our contingency plans and move forward from these disasters, to move forward to even greater things.

Was NASA right or wrong in deciding to continue with the Shuttle programme? History will no doubt offer opinions on this; but they made a choice and followed it through. We can all use our judgement in places, situations and with people. We often feel that things are black and white, that there is a right and wrong. There is also that dual reaction

R – Recognise Results and Mould Your Reality

where things don't always seem black and white; that area of grey that tests our views about justice. Is there justice in our failures? When we take the victim approach then we begin to lose sight of the reality of our world. When we alter that approach we find the hope to continue and reinvent.

Our attitude to events and places around us is really important. We can remain a victim and begrudge others who might succeed or we can regroup within ourselves and step forward and up to the new challenges that we will be presented with. We take back our power of mind and thought by stepping back up and dusting ourselves off. We again reconnect to that spark which doesn't go out, but merely waivers as if a breeze has entered a room. We acknowledge the feeling of failure, but we find renewed power by wanting a new success. Thomas Edison was a man who failed. He failed and he failed and he failed, but he never, ever, ever gave up. For each one of those failures are now forgotten to history. We remember his achievement in inventing the electric light bulb. The miracle of light that he gave us came through his ability to never stop believing in himself and his ideas. He continued to turn his attention to his inventions and he didn't waste his power on his failures. He learned from them, and he refined his ideas, and in his legacy he literally created his divine spark in a tangible form – the light bulb.

Limited thinking stunts our imagination and our growth. We are only limited by what our mind can perceive. If we allow the things that sometimes defeat us to stop us, then we negate and protract our potential. We really can achieve what is in our minds by placing it also in our hearts. Connecting the two gives us strength and direction of purpose. We feel with our hearts what we perceive in our minds and our reality changes. We are guided to things that can help us achieve our desires in our reality. The little girl who watched Man walk on the moon is the adult who walked through the Space Center in awe. That little girl is writing a book, a long held dream but one that is now a reality.

If our purpose is big enough, then we can sustain ourselves through the challenges that we sometimes face. We hold onto the vision of our purpose and we constantly choose and fine tune the direction of our lives. Sometimes that purpose may change and yet we find that it connects us to the greater whole of mankind. Your actions are, and your journey is, consistent with the purpose you choose, those small things that come into your life are seen as the small miracles along the way to find the road to your ultimate purpose. When your resolve to your purpose is firmly fixed, then those pointers and confirmations appear to you in unexplained and unique ways. That slipstream opens up to you and helps guide you ever on. Doing your utmost in all of your tasks, no matter how trivial they seem, leads you to see and find greater things for your life.

It is the slipstream that connects us to all others. We are helped and in turn help others on their path. We are often not conscious of these wider connections, yet they are there for us and like a veil they also protect us when we listen. The intertwining of our endeavours brings about the change that we see in our world. Why is it that some of our greatest minds sit in academic places of learning and encourage and enhance our lives? They do so because they find others who understand and guide them. Why do we sit around the pub with our friends and share our hopes

R – Recognise Results and Mould Your Reality

and dreams? Because we find people who believe in us, who share with us and who guide us. We are drawn to like-minded people and this in turn allows us to grow and assist others in their growth to fulfil their potential and to find their own miracle mindset. Our ancestors lived in tribes and thrived in the community that surrounded them. We are no different today, only that we have so many choices of tribes to join and follow. We have a tribe at work, in our neighbourhood, online, in our church, in our sporting team, in our pub; our choice of tribes is endless. But each tribe connects us to the greater whole. Each tribe enables us to enter the slipstream that others are in and that can help us. Imagine again if there were only one tribe, one humanity, what a peaceful world we would live in.

> *"Imagine all the people, living for today……… You may say I'm a dreamer, but I'm not the only one. I hope some day you'll join us and the world will live as one."*
>
> *John Lennon*

Whenever we find that something wonderful happens in our lives, one of the best things we can do is acknowledge that something wonderful has happened. In our acknowledgment of it, we are showing not just our gratitude but our respect for those wonderful things that come our way. We may not understand how we were given that promotion, or met the man of our dreams, but we nevertheless take the time to wonder and remark at our good fortune. For we don't always have to understand something for it to be our reality; but we can acknowledge that it is our reality and just how grateful we are that it came our way. The child-like quality of wonder allows our imagination to remain with us and enables us to keep those dreams alive in our minds.

> "The most beautiful and profound emotion we can experience is the sensation of the mystical. It is the sower of all true science. He to whom this emotion is a stranger, who can no longer wonder and stand rapt in awe is good as dead." - Albert Einstein

The more we do this and focus on those wonderful things that happen, the less emphasis we place on the failures and on the disasters that we sometimes meet. We begin to realise our potential and we see that our potential is limitless. Our imagination can provide us with the ideas that lead to the new discoveries and ideas of tomorrow. We can be the person in the business who makes suggestions and implements plans to bring about their achievement. We can do this in every part of our lives. That divine spark awaits, the abundance of the universe is there for us all. We can achieve those things we want in life, we just have to connect to the dream we hold and somehow the slipstream enters our world. It's okay to really rejoice when this happens. The feeling of successfully selling your home so you can buy your dream home, is okay. In fact, that joy you feel can only compound for the other dreams you have for your future. That joy does not leave you when times may become a little darker, and that joy will be there again for you in another form to celebrate the successes in your life.

R – Recognise Results and Mould Your Reality

If you could bottle that feeling of joy, hold onto it, return to it, then wouldn't you feel better when and if the darkness descends on you again? Knowing that you can feel that joy in your life gives you hope in your future.

Sometimes our futures don't feel so bright. We can get buffeted by hurdles and challenges. The way to reclaim your dreams in those times is to start with the resolve to never give up. The light bulb moment for Edison took thousands of failures, but his focus stayed on his dream. Allow your focus to stay with your dream. Continue to believe that wonderful things truly do happen and that you can achieve beyond your current limitations. Our focus and clear intention allows us the space to reconnect and to reiterate our goals. Sometimes we need help and that is okay. Allowing our hand to go up and ask for assistance is a sign that we believe in our goal. Asking for assistance is not easy; you can ask the universe for that assistance or you may ask a friend. One thing is sure - that assistance will come to you when you ask. Take the time you need to regroup and refocus. Take the advice you may be given and be thankful for those who have walked ahead of you on the journey. Remember the disasters of others, to recall that sometimes we all are slowed down, but that is not an end to the journey to achieve your goals. Remember too that sometimes when we least expect it, that little miracle shows itself to us to brighten our day. It may be the laughter of a child from up the street in your neighbourhood, it may be the dew on the ground when you first wake to meet the day, it may be the eyes of your loved one smiling as you wake, but it will have meaning to your world and it will be that miracle that shines from the darkness and that allows us to continue on our journey.

When we ask for something, it may not come to us immediately. Sometimes it feels like we never get what we want from life, and we step into the mode of the victim. It is times like these that we need to suspend our disbelief and ask for help anyway. If we remain open to the possibility that we will get the assistance that we seek, then help comes to us from often unexpected sources. Sometimes we get an immediate response to something that is troubling us and these little things add up to the wider miracle that is the world in which we live.

You may be reading this and thinking that is all very well for you, but my life has never been anything but trouble. By starting to change your attitude and thinking and moving towards others who don't have those troubles, your life may begin to see some new horizons. The people that you hang around with have a huge effect on your life. Why not read a biography of someone you admire and enjoy reading about their challenges and successes? Look into their life and see where there are parallels with your own. What did that person do when times got tough? Talk to people that you admire and ask the same questions. What would they do in a particular situation? Seek out someone who has been through a similar situation and seek their guidance.

Find a coach in the true sense of the word. Someone who presents an image you respect and admire. They may not be a formal coach, but you will be surprised at the effect this may have on your world. A role model can keep us on track, they can change our reality and they can allow us to hold onto the image of ourselves that may be fading with disappointment and regret. They may just remind us to never, ever, ever give up. But remember to thank them

R – Recognise Results and Mould Your Reality

and acknowledge them and treasure them in your life. For one day, you may find yourself in their shoes and all at once it is a great privilege, a great honour and a great burden to assist a fellow traveller, but one that is a mark of your life and your achievements, no matter how you perceive them. And back to NASA for one last thought, the tragedy that was Challenger didn't prevent other tragedies from occurring, but it did spur on the space program and today, the reverence for those lost astronauts and others like them empowers the dreamers in us all to reach for the stars and to succeed in our dreams.

ACTION STEPS:

1. Write a list of your mistakes. Work out ways that you could have avoided them.
2. Write a list of your achievements – celebrate the things that matter.
3. Ask for help if you need it.
4. Offer to help someone else.
5. Acknowledge the connections, the people that helped you get this far – write a list and thank them.
6. Read a biography or autobiography of someone you admire – learn from them.
7. Write out your ultimate dream and hold onto it when times get tough.

"Mystery creates wonder and wonder is the basis of man's desire to understand." – Neil Armstrong

Paul Barratt's Thoughts on Miracles

Paul Barratt

PAUL BARRATT'S THOUGHTS ON MIRACLES

If you had met me a few years ago, you would have seen that I was out of breath and had a very blue tinge to my skin. I was born with a congenital heart defect. When I was very young, I was told I wouldn't be around for very long. As you may find while reading this, I'm not the sort of person who would just lie down and accept that news as a fact. Many of the things I have done have been in the face of great adversity. I'm a father, an IT consultant, an author, a trader on the Foreign Exchange market, a motivational speaker, as well as doing many other things, but most importantly I have a passion for life. I make a difference in different communities around Australia and in 2010, I'm starting to make an impact in communities around the world. I am working in different ways to improve the lives of other people.

I believe a miracle is the intersection of dreams, passions and actions. I am the cause of miracles and not at the effect of circumstances. In some ways, my life has been miraculous, but I've always been looking for opportunities and creating the possibility of having miracles arise.

> "You want to see a miracle, son? Be the miracle."
> – Morgan Freeman (God) from Bruce Almighty

For me, mindset is the building block of what actually creates the miracles in our lives. Having a strong mindset with big dreams, strong beliefs and determination, can create extraordinary outcomes for you and people around you. Another way of looking at it is, that with a little effort, we go from the ordinary to the EXTRA-ORDINARY...

My determination has been a big factor in my successes when growing up. I believe that it has been my determination that has allowed me to move forward in spite of adverse circumstances. Having said that, you need to understand that there have been many times when things didn't go well and what was happening in my world really got me down. It is at these times that I have had to dig deep down and find that small miraculous thread of hope that allowed me to move forward in spite of myself, and in spite of my circumstances. It is amazing what you can create when you have a positive outlook. Determination is something that has been with me from my very early years.

If you are continually looking outwards, you'll see extraordinary things that other people are creating. I believe that miracles start from within. If you're prepared to look in and take action in your own life, then you can have miracles come into being for yourself. In doing this and taking action you can see and create miracles for other people at the same time. Other people will be inspired by what you are doing and will take action for themselves. The advantage of this, I think, is if you have a group of people believing in the same thing, then miracles can arise in the same direction for everyone. This can provide a greater impact and thus give a much larger outcome than an individual working on their own.

Another way of having miracles arise on a large scale is for one person to take action, and have other people see it as an opportunity, and for them to take action and build on what was originally created. I believe this is what creates some of the largest changes socially, environmentally and inspirationally in our world. They may not be viewed as miracles at the time, but on reflection the final outcome, I believe, is where some of the largest changes come into our world. One of the best examples I know of where action has been taken on a large scale is Earth Hour. Todd Sampson (CEO of Leo Burnett, one of Australia's top creative advertising agencies) is the co-creator of the Earth Hour initiative. From a simple idea, that others said would not work, he and many others involved have created an environmental awareness that started in Sydney and has now expanded on a world wide scale. Earth Hour has now been recognised as one the best ideas in the world. In 2009, 1 billion people around the world participated in Earth Hour making it the biggest environment movement in history. For me, this is one of those changes that has impacted the world socially, environmentally and inspirationally. The result can be viewed as a miracle as so many are now involved in such a positive way.

When I look at some of the things that I create and do in my life I am often reminded of this quote:

> "A person with a new idea is a crank until the idea succeeds"
> - Mark Twain

I look at the miracles in my life, the ideas that have gone on to inspire others, the events that have had an impact on the lives of those around me as well as my own and I can often recall someone saying at the start that I was a little nuts for even thinking about taking some things on.

The flow of miracles around me and in my life is like having things, feelings and events that I've created and other people

Paul Barratt's Thoughts on Miracles

have built on and moved forward with, which in turn has had an impact on not just my local communities but extended communities as well.

> "There is no good idea that cannot be improved on if you only allow it to grow and give it the wings to fly."
> - Paul Barratt 2005

It was about two weeks after I was released from the hospital, after having a heart and lung transplant that I told the doctors I was doing the City to Surf Fun Run. To put this into perspective, until I had the transplant I had never participated in any physical activity because I did not have the physical capability to even walk up a set of stairs with out becoming breathless. As you can imagine the "idea" of doing the City to Surf, just after the transplant, made the doctors sit up and think maybe this is not such a good idea. I felt so good that I still went ahead and did it. That I was going to do the City to Surf a matter of weeks after the transplant was a miracle that touched, moved and inspired many people. In fact, I created such a wave of inspiration that the hospital and the Heart and Lung Transplant Foundation joined me and put together a team to do the City to Surf. That particular year we had the best equipped team in the event because we had doctors, nurses, wheelchairs, oxygen, orderlies and a physiotherapist, as well as well as some of my friends, family and other transplant patients.

The best outcome for me is that each year since, the hospital has had a transplant group that goes into the event. In this way, what I created from that one idea was inspirational, a miracle for them. It was a miracle for me as well, as until the moment I crossed the finish line of the City to Surf, it had only ever been a dream, a hope and a wish. It was completely extraordinary to me that, combined with opportunity and action, I had been able to complete something that I had never been able to do before.

That one idea, that one action, has affected different communities in an ongoing way. It has made a difference and inspired others to look for miracles in their own lives. As an example of what I mean, it was couple of years after my first City to Surf that another patient joined in who inspired me and others. He participated in the City to Surf carrying his ventricular assist device (VAD), also known as a heart pump (a mechanical device that helps pump blood from the heart to the rest of your body). From what I had created the flow of miracles continued.

Successful living goes back to what I think is the building block of miracles - dreams, passion, action and mindset. Everybody has their ups and downs, but it's a matter of having the mindset and the passion to keep moving forward no matter how dark things look. For all of my upbeat moments, you need to know that there are times when there has been absolute despair where I just can't think what to do. It is at those times that I become the most creative.

The greatest miracle for me is the one yet to come. I think you should never stop looking for or creating miracles in your life or the lives of people around you. I am continually creating new opportunities and new ways of being while looking for ways I can help and improve another's world or life.

Having said that, there are miracles that I treasure each and every day. The top of that list is the miracle of my own life. I love being able to see the difference I make in the lives of people around me just because I am still here contributing, creating and taking action in different areas of life.

I am blessed to have people that have always been with me in my journey of life. They have seen the miracles that have been around me as I have grown up. Frequently they have been closely involved or the source of the miracles that have impacted my life. These people include my parents, my family and many very good friends. My greatest supporter and inspiration over the last 25 years has been my wife, Joanne. For me, Joanne is one of the most extraordinary people I know. Joanne is not just my wife but she is my best friend and she gives me support, balance and guidance on a daily basis. Joanne feeds me both spiritually and emotionally. It is with all of these elements that I am able to create and have miracles arise. With some of the things I do Joanne is very patient and understanding, even on occasions when I am sure she just can't believe what I am creating or intending to do.

Joanne has given me what I consider is the greatest miracle in my life. That miracle is my son Chris. Chris is a miracle for us as, due to my health challenges and other factors, Joanne and I were never sure that we could have children. I can tell you that the day he was born, and I had the privilege of holding him in my arms, in that moment I was clear that I was holding a real miracle. Joanne and I have been blessed to be able to watch him grow up and guide him to be the passionate young man that he is now. I am proud to be able to say that Chris is not just my son, but also my friend. Chris and Joanne often join me on my adventures that create a difference in so many other lives.

It has been a miracle that I lived to be 45 before I had to have the heart and lung transplant and it was my passion for life and taking action to live life as best I could that had got me that far. Other miracles I see more as a gift from other people, for example - my heart and lung transplant and how successful that was, is a miracle that was created by the extraordinary and talented medical team who were responsible for my transplant. It's a result of their work that I now have the miraculous life that I do. I guess no matter how you look at it, I'm just very, very lucky and I have the privilege of living a miraculous life each and every day.

> "We don't accomplish anything in this world alone...
>
> Whatever happens is the result of the whole tapestry of one's life
>
> and all the weavings of individual threads from one to another
>
> that creates something"
>
> - Sandra Day O'Connor

You may well ask what my journey of life had been like. I was born with a congenital heart defect. I was diagnosed with my heart condition at about five years of age and my parents were told that if I lived to be nine years of age, I would be very lucky. I made it past nine (I am sure that Mum and Dad thought that was a bit of a miracle) and the doctors then said that I probably wouldn't make it to 15. They were nearly right. When I was 12 I became extremely ill and nearly died and spent a week in a coma. But I fought back to give life another go. Surviving that was a miracle. I think eventually my doctors gave up predicting my demise when I was about 21. I continued to make the most of everything I did. When I was 45 the doctors said that I'd

Paul Barratt's Thoughts on Miracles

gone into heart failure and, at that time, the prognosis was very dire. They said I needed a heart-lung transplant and they also said that I needed to go to the eastern states for the operation as, at that time, they didn't perform Heart Lung transplants in Perth. One of my specialists even went so far as to say that my condition was so severe that by the time they organised for me to go to Melbourne it was likely that I would already be dead.

This was one of those times when I hit the depths of despair. I remember a day in hospital where I was alone. I was lying there and feeling very sorry for myself. But in the depths of despair I re-created my dream and my passion for life and started to take action. I started having conversations with people. I wasn't going to give up that easily and I started conversations with as many people as I could (doctors are people too). I was determined that I would live long enough to go to Melbourne if needed, but I also started to create the possibility of having the transplant right here in Perth. I took action. It was action and that single-minded determination that had the miracle occur. It was that intersection of dreams, passion and action that had the reality created of a Heart and Lung Transplant program in Perth. It was that intersection between dreams, passion and action that had me become the first person listed in Western Australia for a Heart and Lung transplant.

I remember when Joanne and I sat down with my favourite surgeon (any surgeon who performs the operation that saves your life automatically becomes a favourite). It was during that meeting with Dr Robert Larbalestier that he started the Heart Lung Transplant program. The Tuesday after, I was officially listed as the first possible Heart and Lung transplant recipient. Another miracle is that only four days later, I had that all important call to the hospital where I was given my new heart and lungs. It was a miracle, as I didn't have to wait for three, six, or twelve months or more like most transplant patients usually have to wait. I was very lucky, it was a miracle and I thank my donor family each and every day.

The other "people part" of this miracle were the 12-person surgical team led by cardiothoracic surgeon Dr Robert Larbalestier. The entire process was a huge team effort involving surgeons, respiratory physicians, cardiologists, intensive care physicians, specialist anaesthetists, theatre technicians, nurses, physiotherapists and occupational therapists, dieticians, social workers, ward staff, clinical immunologists and infection disease consultants.

Just to remind you of the start of a quote earlier -

"We don't accomplish anything in this world alone..."

Another miracle that came out of the transplant is how quickly I recovered. It is not uncommon for Heart and Lung transplant recipients to be in hospital for months after the transplant. Again, with the same passion, determination and action, I created the possibility that I would recover quickly. It was the third day after the transplant that I told my doctors what day I would be discharged and go home.

The day I had chosen was 17 days after my transplant. The reason I had was that it was Joanne's birthday and as I was in hospital that was the best gift I could think of to give her. So using the old formula (the intersection of dreams, passion and action) it was clear I had the dream, I definitely had the passion so all that was left was for me to take action. I took every action that any of my medical team asked of me and in many cases I did more than was asked of me so I could ensure my recovery. The result was I was released on Joanne's birthday and I spent the night at home with a celebratory dinner. A celebration of her day and my discharge from hospital - at the time it was a perfect birthday gift. Being discharged from hospital in just 17 days was a miracle. However, it was the fact that I took all the actions required that made the miracle arise.

If you're going to be sitting back looking for a miracle, you will be doing that all your life.

To have miracles appear:

<u>You have to have a dream.</u>

<u>You have to have a passion.</u>

<u>You have to take action.</u>

> *"When the time comes,
> Ideas move rapidly taking you to a destination
> that you may not always intend"*
> *– Paul Barratt*

Sometimes, when you have a dream and a passion and you take action, you may find that the result is different from what you had set out to achieve. The interesting thing is that, at these times when you sit back and reflect, quite often you see that it was the right result after all. I always find it interesting that in my life I may not always get everything I want, but what I do get as a result is PERFECT at the time. The important thing here is that you need to be in action, doing something, in order to get any result. If you are not in action in your life, nothing will ever happen. There is NO chance of a miracle arising.

For me, life, and that's any life, is a miracle. My health today is still a miracle for me. I wouldn't say my health is 100%, but I am better now than I ever was before the transplant. The miracle for me now is that I can create and have an impact in different communities and the lives of the people that I meet.

In some ways, miracles are just every day things that happen that can improve the lives of people around me. Just being able to do that, is a miracle. Some of the changes and successes that I see are what makes the journey worthwhile. In some of the areas that I have worked in, I have made a difference, including the bigger things like serving on the board of Heart Kids WA or serving on the board of the Heart and Lung Transplant Foundation. I have done advisory work with several other charities. I have created projects that have raised awareness and much needed money for many different charities and other groups. Because of this I have inspired many people to take action in their own life and contribute to communities in many different ways. Some of the projects that I create are on a scale that touches and inspires many different communities. For example, I am currently working with the Lung Institute of Western Australia (LIWA). The project is to ride a mountain bike 498km along the Munda Biddi trail in Western Australia with my son. Fortunately Joanne will be there supporting me in the bike ride.

> "Behind every great man is a woman rolling her eyes"
> - Jim Carey (Bruce) from Bruce Almighty

Having said that, the bike ride is just part of the outcome. In the process of the project, we are raising awareness for LIWA as well as much needed funds for patient support and lung research. We have generated an amazing amount of media coverage so that the work of the Institute is now much better

Paul Barratt's Thoughts on Miracles

known. We have raised funds for research, we have impacted the transplant patient community by showing what is possible after a transplant and we have impacted Lung patient communities, as well as many different country communities by showing them a way they can contribute and make a difference. We have also raised awareness for the world class Munda Biddi Mountain bike trail as well as many other communities along the way. The point here is that when you start something you can never be sure who will be touched or influenced by what you create and do. This project, like many similar projects, can become an inspiration to many people. In the process, other people can see an opportunity to make it better and in turn touch, move and inspire others.

It is possible that the ride I am doing this year will inspire someone to create an event that will further enhance the work and fund raising capabilities of the Lung Institute of Western Australia.

You never know if or when you can make a difference or create miracles in another's world. So it is important to always be in the conversation and looking for opportunities. Several years ago, I went to a Heart Kids camp and in many ways I was the odd one out. I didn't have a child with a heart problem. I wasn't on the medical staff and I wasn't really a kid any more (I understand that when you are 46 you are supposed to be an adult). I was an "adult" heart kid. One night I was asked to stand up and talk to the kids about my journey through life as a heart kid. For many kids, it was like, okay, there really is hope for me - there really is chance I can do lots of stuff in my life. Here's this guy who is 46 and he's standing up here and he had a heart condition so here I am- 12, 13, 14- and things aren't that bad. I can live a long life. I can get out and do things. For me having that sort of response was inspiring. Some of those kids I still talk to. They follow what

I am doing and I am inspired by what they are doing with their lives and how they are taking on the challenges that they have to face.

Another area where I work with kids is as a public speaker. I talk in several schools and other groups. There is one school that I have spoken at for a few years, a high school in Western Australia. I am usually known as the guy with the heart thing. When I am there, I usually answer any questions they may think of and along the way I talk to them about never giving up, being determined, going out and getting what you want, and most importantly making the most of your life. It has an impact on those kids each and every year. After I have done one of these talks I get letters back from each of the kids. Now I know that it's probably a teaching outcome to have the kids write the letters, but what the young adults write in those letters is not a teaching outcome. What goes in those letters is stuff from the heart. When I read those letters I see that I have had an impact on each and every one of those kids. There was one letter I remember where a young woman (15) said 'The teacher made me stay, I didn't want to because I thought you were a bit of a loser' - a good start to the letter but it continued on - 'but I'm glad I did stay because I learned about being tolerant, being compassionate.' She then went on and listed a number of things that she saw in her life from what I had to deal with in my life. At the end of the letter she said "Because you came, this is what I'm going to do to help my Mum... This is what I'm going to do for me.... and this is how I am going to be different to my friends..."

Now that showed me what an impact I had on her. It was a completely unexpected result. She was considered to be "below average" and had more than just the usual challenges to deal with. I saw it as a real miracle that she was able to get so much from my talk. The teacher was surprised at the response and for

Paul Barratt's Thoughts on Miracles

me it was inspiring that she saw a different way of going about things.

Sometimes the kids at this school made me feel like a rock star. After one of my talks, one of the kids (who had rarely been to school that year), came up to me and asked for my autograph. He got so much from my talk that I had inspired him to do something more with his life. I understand that he attended school more often after the talk - another unexpected result. Whenever I can, I try to touch, move and inspire people to do more and create more in their own lives and in doing so make a difference to others.

When I am talking with people I can see, hear and feel that what I'm doing is the right thing. As to whether it's a miracle? Only time will tell. You see, whether it's a little miracle or a big miracle, you don't know until it's finished. Just as the example I gave you with the 15 year old woman. I went to the school to give a talk and answer questions. At the time I had no idea what sort of an impact I would have on her or her class mates until I received the letters. If you like, it was the verification that I had an impact, that I had made a difference, that what I am doing is worthwhile. In this way I am creating little miracles in other people's lives as I go.

> *"In order to be a realist you must believe in miracles."*
> *- David Ben-Gurion*

To look at the anatomy of a miracle would be to look at what effect dreams, passions and actions have on other people. Sometimes I ask the question "What positive difference have I made?" I believe that each and every day, every person can and does have a miraculous life and that they can create miracles both small and large while on the journey of life. Too often, we get caught up looking for the so-called big miracles and as a result we miss all the little miracles along the way. When it comes to really big miracles, Jesus is the only one who has ever been able to walk on water.

> *"Dreams and passion pass into the reality with action. From the results of the actions the dream can be created again and miracles arise."*
>
> *– Paul Barratt.*

For all the other miracles in life, we can create miracles in our own lives in such a way that we can make a difference not just in our world but also in another's. Sometimes the joy and the exultation that we experience can make us feel like we can fly. When we experience this, it can appear to be a miracle for another person because it is so different from their own experience of life at that time.

A miracle is being able to create something that has an impact on another's life so that the world's a better place for them and their experience of life is better too. It's the gift that you can give each and every day. Sometimes the gift that you give is so profound that you feel like anything is possible. In fact, I believe that you can be, do and have anything you want in your life so long as you are prepared to create what is needed in another's world. In sharing what I do and how I can go about it, I often see other people creating and moving forward in their own lives. This is

Paul Barratt's Thoughts on Miracles

something that we all can do.

Prior to my transplant a lot of the time I was too busy just living in survival mode. The times when I turned my focus on other people and creating something in their lives, not only would I make a difference to them, but also I would make a difference in my life because for that time I was not focused on what I had to deal with. In this way I was able to have an impact in other people's communities and in doing so made a difference to myself.

I look for and see miracles each and every day. I don't have to look very far to find what could be seen as a big miracle. There are a lot of people that I work with that create miracles all the time. They make a difference to other people and other communities.

I believe that miracles are more than just recovering from diseases or disasters. Twelve months after my Heart Lung transplant, Joanne was diagnosed with breast cancer. Here we are a several years after my transplant, a few years after Joanne's diagnosis and she is now cancer free. That may be viewed as a miracle, but for me the real miracle that I like to watch each and every year is the extraordinary impact Joanne has on the children she teaches. It is amazing how over the course of twelve months, she has the privilege of seeing them grow from children into young people who see and feel the possibility of life, who see the excitement of life and learning and they do this with every waking moment. It's these sorts of miracles that I like to look for.

When it comes to miracles and being able to create something new, from what has already been created, there is one person who has made a difference that helped create a miracle in my life, a lady by the name of Yvonne Bali (Cox). Yvonne is a Lung Transplant recipient. After her transplant, Yvonne worked tirelessly to have the Lung Transplant unit started in Perth. It was Yvonne's dream, passion and action over many years that had the Lung Transplant unit started in Western Australia for the benefit of others. After many years, Yvonne continues to work in the Heart and Lung Transplant Foundation.

It was from what Yvonne created that made it possible for me to have the miracle occur in my life. It was being able to build on what she created that the Heart and Lung transplant program started and for me to be the first person to benefit. That is one of my miracles.

If Yvonne didn't have that dream and passion or take the actions to create the Foundation then I am very sure that I may not have been able to have my heart and lung transplant in Perth. My miracle was created from another's dream, passion and action, allowing me to have the lifesaving operation I did.

In this way, what you create may only seem like a small thing today, but you never know what may happen or who will make your dream bigger and better than you could possibly imagine.

That is why I tend to look for the little miracles along the way; the little pieces of creation, the small steps to a larger miracle that benefits many.

I know that I'm truly blessed to have many people in my life who give and receive miracles. As a parting message, I would go back to where we started. Miracles are the intersection of dreams, passion and action. If you have the dreams, the passion and take action, then the EXTRA-ORDINARY can arise.

> *"The world has the habit of making room for the man whose actions show that he knows where he is going."*
>
> Napoleon Hill

A - Attitude of Gratitude

A – ATTITUDE OF GRATITUDE

> *"It's all a dream world and gratitude is the essence. Gratitude has a ripple effect in all areas of our lives. And our real power in life is awakened through gratitude and it's effect called love."* – Dr John Demartini

In other chapters I have referred to an attitude of gratitude and how that helps to bring more miracles into our lives, how it helps us to enter the slipstream. It is important for us to pay attention to this perhaps most of all, as it helps us to truly see the blessings that we have already been given in our lives. Being grateful for what we have in terms of our body and what it does for us every day. Being grateful for our family, our friends, for a roof over our heads, for the tiniest of things that we own to the greatest mansion. When we do this we allow ourselves to focus our hearts. Saying thank you for someone's kindness or for their service does two things. Firstly, it shows the person that we appreciate them, even if we are paying them for their role, and secondly, it reminds us that we have been given something that serves our needs. If we string together all the people and things that we need to thank in a day, we could spend a lot of time. Writing down our thanks in a journal allows us to see just how much we can be truly grateful for. It also has the effect of reminding us in our low ebb points that we have so much to be grateful for and whatever is happening to us at that moment will also pass.

One of the best places to start in this gratitude journal is with ourselves. We are often our harshest critic and giving thanks

A – Attitude of Gratitude

for our being is a truly miraculous thing. We forget that life is a journey and through that journey we learn different things, not just about ourselves but other people and things around us. We are all learning and sometimes we interfere and intervene in others' lives. Being able to forgive ourselves for these mistakes, and then being able to forgive others, frees us to be able to accept all that we can offer and that others can offer us. If we can embrace this wholeheartedly, then we allow more gifts to come to us. Those gifts aren't always in a material form. So embrace the small things that make you feel great.

We are all connected, but we are also unique. We have different dreams and desires, but we walk this world together. If we can accept that point of difference, then we can learn to accept that not everyone is going to agree with us, that not everyone is going to share our hopes. If we enter into that mindset, then we can begin to realise that those differences and dreams that we hold go to make up the melting pot of our world; that we are shaping the world in which we live and that we can be grateful for others' ideas and contributions to our whole. When we do this, we start to attract a whole lot more of the things that we want. When we focus with a positive approach, then we begin to respect others' opinions and ideas and they in turn return that respect to us. We begin to see how we can have greater influence and input into our own lives and share in helping others do the same for their lives. We find that the divine matrix will connect our sparks at times when we need them and people suddenly appear in our lives to help at certain points, and that fluidity is truly miraculous. The slipstream carries us all and connects us when we take action.

> *"Human beings can alter their lives by altering the attitudes of their mind."* – William James

Our attitude is important, not only for focusing on gratitude but by combining this with a positive mindset. Our attitude is adaptable. We can choose to be in a bad mood or we can look at that mood and replace it with a brighter and sunnier one. The day around us will respond to this change in attitude and by having this check and balance to our attitude we can go a long way to being the change that we want to see in the world. We can't always be complaining and expect others to respond to us in a positive way. They will only see the negativity and respond to that, but if you start to smile and share some other more positive stories and events with them you begin to tip the balance. Your home life and your workplace can become less hostile by checking on your own emotions and bringing balance back to your outlook.

Fear is one emotion that can debilitate us and shift us from our goals. If we truly begin to love unconditionally and replace that fear with love, then we begin to dissolve fear whenever it rises within us. For fear comes from a lack of trust and, when we love and trust, we begin to see the slipstream enter our lives and show us some truly wonderful moments. Love and trust thrive in an environment where there is faith; that faith can be a belief in God or in the universe or in one's self. For faith in oneself is really faith in God. For if we are created in God's image, then we have nothing to fear. We are given everything that we need and it is there for us to call upon. We just have to remember to call upon our resilience, our inner spark, when we need it.

As we begin to believe this in our hearts and our mind, then we begin to see that we start to attract the things in life that we want. If we change our focus to those things we want instead of the broken record of woe and the things that go wrong, then we start to see the slipstream shift in our favour. Focus on the things that you want, focus with all your intention. Apply that

A – Attitude of Gratitude

intention as if the thing is already in your life. Add the emotion and hope that goes with attaining your dream; how does it feel? Visualise the moment in time when your dream is a reality. Do this every day and give thanks for your dream. The passion behind the visualisation adds to the formula to bring things, people and events to support your dream. Believe it is real and you will invoke your reality, you will achieve it. Put a timeframe on this and you have set the wheels in motion, but remember to believe that you have already received.

> *"In the arena of human life, the honours and reward fall to those who show their good qualities in action." - Aristotle*

The more we give thanks for those things that we have, the more we are given. Saying thank you is the building block upon which we step in our chosen direction. The more we receive, the more we are able to do; and the more we are able to do, the more we can give thanks for. We are then able to bring happiness, not just to ourselves and our immediate family but to others who may not have the opportunities. We begin to see the slipstream working and we know that we are on the right path. We begin to harness the power and things shift almost before we have thought about them. We are given opportunities that, at one point, seemed only for a 'special few'. The thing is we are all that "special few". We all have that divine spark within us and we can all choose to call on it to provide us with strength and determination. Saying thank you for the tough times and for the good times, for the lessons and the triumphs, only serves to build our resistance and our resilience as we step to reach new goals and new challenges.

Our attitude is like our compass. It points true when we are on the right track. It guides us back to our path and it enables us to move through the darkness. Our attitude is like a lighthouse through the darkness. If we have an attitude of gratitude and one of forgiveness, then we find that it is returned to us and people will go out of their way to help us find our path, move beyond the darkness that sometimes befalls us and allow us to feel safe and sound. We all have those moments where life seems unfair, where our challenges seem insurmountable, but when you begin to talk with others you learn that they have had something similar or they have responded to a challenge in a way that could also work for you and that is where our connection truly comes to light. Each of us has experiences that, whilst unique, can also serve as a guide for another's journey. When we remember this, we find that we are not alone, that we can find inspiration in our journey and the journey of others. Our radar sometimes brings into our orbit those people who best lead us through the darkness until we find the resolve and strength again to continue with our own resources. For it is not our resources that fail us, it is just that we forget that we have everything that we need within us.

The attitude of gratitude is almost like a bank: the more we do it, the more we save. The more we save, the greater our contribution and the more we are able to call on if we reach a point of difficulty. The slipstream comes to us and flows for us when we really begin to show our thanks and clear away our doubts and our negative emotions. We then begin to see more and more of the small things, the small miracles and the big ones flow to us and through us. For we also begin to have the means to help others connect to the slipstream and bring the flow into their lives.

A – Attitude of Gratitude

> "What you focus on expands, and when you focus on the goodness in your life, you create more of it. Opportunities, relationships, even money flowed my way when I learned to be grateful no matter what happened in my life." – Oprah Winfrey

We all forget that this world is open to us and that is why we still are amazed at the stories of miraculous survivals and events. When we apply our wish or desire with unshaken faith and focus, then the miracle becomes our reality. I have spoken with several people in this book who have had miraculous recoveries from cancer and life threatening illness. The thing to remember is to seek the appropriate medical assistance and set about enhancing your own outcome. It is really important to abandon negative thinking when talking about flowing miracles into your life. It is also important not to try to grasp onto to the miracle like it is the only thing available to you. Move in the direction of what you want to achieve and expect that it will happen. Being in this flow allows things that will help you achieve your desire move toward you.

In our lives we are sometimes told that ambitious people don't have good ethics, or they are not to be trusted. Just wait for a moment and reanalyse your thinking around that statement. Ambitious people don't always think only of themselves. Ambition leads people to strive for greater things and to achieve greater things in their lives. If Thomas Edison had not had ambition, we might still be sitting in the dark and you would now be struggling to read my handwriting or perhaps snoring while I told you my story. For it is this ambition coupled with the will to achieve that brings us to meet the slipstream. Our intention is important and our willingness to go the extra mile is necessary, but the legacy that we can leave is lasting and can create an impact so as to allow the future generations to work from a different level. This level is in not just in great achievements but in the humanity that witnesses these achievements. For our development is not merely in acquiring personal goals and items we want, our development comes in being able to share things that might assist someone else, and for this we can be truly grateful.

Sometimes, when we think of the potential that we all have, we pull back and become frightened. We think that someone else will do it, that someone else is more qualified, that someone else knows more than we do. We can allow this to defeat us before we begin to live our dreams. We can restrict our outcomes by convincing ourselves that someone else is the one to do this or that; that it is not our role. That may be true, but if you are strongly driven to do something, to achieve something, and you put all the things suggested into action, then the sky truly is the limit.

Visualise what you want in your life and affirm each day that these changes are already yours. Reinforce in your subconscious what you want and begin to show your subconscious you have already accepted that it is your reality. When we start to do this, we find that somehow things are directed to us to help us reach the destination of our dreams. When we begin to clarify in our mind what we want, the slipstream of miracles comes to us. We have to put the step of action into our lives and we are met with assistance and support. Our attitude is everything and a positive and humble attitude of gratitude will progress us beyond our perceived limits and we might just find ourselves living our dreams – what a concept.

A – Attitude of Gratitude

ACTION STEPS:

1. Start your gratitude journal if you have not already done so.
2. Write in it every day or review what you have written at least once a day.
3. Forgive yourself for mistakes.
4. Forgive others for mistakes made against you.
5. Focus on the positive events in your day.
6. Visualise the outcomes you want, add emotion and passion – do this every day; touch, taste and feel the outcome as if it is already with you.
7. Offer to assist someone.

> "Humanity cannot forget its dreamers. It cannot let their ideas fade and die. It lives in them. It knows them as realities which it shall one day see and know. Composers, sculptors, painters, poets, prophets and sages are the makers of tomorrow. These are the architects of heaven."
> - John Donne

Michael's Thoughts on Miracles

MICHAEL'S THOUGHTS ON MIRACLES

> *"The miracles on earth are the laws of heaven."*
> *- Jean Paul*

We started off our lymphoma website with people coming up to us and saying things like, "Geez Michael, you look great, you look better than you ever have before. What did you do? What was your secret to surviving cancer?" So we often thought about writing a book about my story. And it wasn't until we went to an internet course where the true realisation came about. Daryl and Andrew Grant put together a course to do with membership sites. We tossed around a few ideas and it just hit home – "Hey, why not tell my story about the cancer survival?" I wanted to give those people the answers, not just the people that asked, but anyone else who may be affected by this illness or know someone who's affected. So we incorporated all things like your physical, mental and spiritual side, in other words a holistic approach to surviving the cancer.

It was long ago thought of, but never came to fruition, because synchronicity wasn't there, we weren't ready and the universe tested us and said "Well, are you gonna do this, aren't you gonna do this?" And all of a sudden we found the right combination, put it all together and it happened.

A miracle (by my definition anyway) is something we see in every day. Each day that we wake up, each day that we breathe, each time that we see a flower bloom, are they not all miracles? We go to sleep at night not having to wonder how our heart's going to beat or the breath that we take, or the cells replenishing

Michael's Thoughts on Miracles

overnight and all the other wonderful things, so all these are miracles. When you go and have a look in the Dictionary under the word miracle, a lot of the time they say words like Divine intervention, the unexpected, statistically unlikely to happen but nonetheless a beneficial result. So I truly believe there is more to it that just what we see with the eyes. There is a divine intervention at play there. When we reconnect with that spiritual side, we start to see the synchronicity between the spiritual side of us and the physical side of us.

There is a divine presence, call it God, call it universal intelligence, call it whatever you want, but there is a divine presence there, and it does intervene with our everyday life. We put the thoughts out there and it just synchronises with those thoughts and it gives us that manifestation, that begins first and foremost with our thoughts.

I connect with this every single day of my life – just by getting up, just by witnessing the sunshine, just by witnessing a flower in bloom, which in itself is a miracle. But more so, in every aspect of my physical life – as far as having a child, as far as having a wonderful relationship, as far as having a beautiful house to live in all began with a thought first and foremost until it manifested into what it is today.

Yes, it does begin with a thought; but having said that, a lot of people believe "Oh, if I think it, it will just manifest into fruition." I don't think it's as easy as that. It's not just by the thought, it's by the feelings. A lot of people think, "I want to get rich. I want to have $10,000 or $10,000,000 in my account." Then they forever spend the rest of their life wondering "Well, why hasn't it happened yet, why isn't this happening?" If they're not happy with what they've got at present, for instance they might have a bank account of $20,000 or $2,000 and think "Oh my god, is that all I've got?" Then they're not in line, or not in synchronicity with their thoughts and feelings. This is also important to have, because if your feelings aren't aligned, you're not going to manifest that which is pertinent to you and miracles won't happen in that respect because you're not in line with the universe.

If we look at miracles, and how they manifest, my experience with the cancer issue 12 years ago, was my greatest miracle of survival. I was given up for dead twice, I went up and saw the light, through the tunnel, but again I came out. I was given a very slim chance of survival by the doctors and those around me. All this time, I truly believed that I would survive, I internalised it, I felt it, I visualised it and I acted upon my beliefs of what I should do to bring the fact into realisation.

Seeing the light was quite a wonderful experience and one I truly wish to embrace again because it was just the most beautiful, overwhelming, peaceful, elated feeling. I went into a coma, an induced coma as part of my experience with the lymphoma cancer, and during that time I physically felt that I had left my body, that I was looking down on my body. I could see everything, I could see everyone. I couldn't touch, I couldn't feel anything, but I was looking down on my body. Then all of a sudden I went through a vortex – it's a tunnel of bright light and it just spirals around and around and around and around, and it's just the most beautiful feeling ever, it's peaceful and elating. And when I stopped, or came to the end, I experienced what my mother and father had always taught me throughout my younger years, through the Bible, that you will be greeted at the pearly gates by St Peter and the angels and that's exactly what happened. I guess that's what happens to most people – it's your belief, your teachings from an early age, otherwise it'd be overwhelming. I was greeted by the angels and told quite specifically that I had two choices now: "You can either stay up here, we'll give you a secret, a safe secret that you had when you were young - you were too young to remember what that was, or too young to make sense of it all." That's the purpose of life, to grow and come to realisations eventually. They said "Or, you can come back down to complete your journey, if you've got some unfinished business to do, or you can stay up here and we'll give you that secret." Now, I chose to come down and I said to them "Well I have got some unfinished business, I believe I still have a purpose." So before coming down my whole life flashed before me on a screen - the past, the present, the future; all the experiences I had, all the people that I had associated with, friends, family, all the things that I had done, all the things that I hadn't done. There's no punishment, there's no feeling of embarrassment or anything like that, it's just pure love, unconditional love. And then I spiralled right back down, through the same tunnel again. And I went back to where I left off – I was looking at my body from up above and it took a good three days to reconnect with that physical body. In that time, I was stuck between heaven and earth, as they say. Not knowing how to reconnect with the body is the greatest fear, I guess, from a physical perspective. When I did reconnect with the body, it was just like a bit of a wake up call, somebody jabbing you with a sharp needle of some sort and I realised I was back in the physical body again.

It took me a good month, month and a half I suppose, to realise exactly where I was. Because of all the drugs I was given during my episode, amnesia drugs and what have you, it took me a whole month to realise. Barbara, my wife, had to back-track a bit and tell me exactly what happened as I had no idea. I knew that I was awake, I knew that I was in the hospital, but I thought that I was manifesting everything about me. If you can just imagine, you close your eyes and you think about things like "Oh geez, I wish my wife was here with me now," and then you open your eyes and there she is, she's standing next to you and you think "Oh God, where am I, you know I'm manifesting things from thin air." I thought the whole dialogue I was making up and everything around me was distorted. Big things were smaller, or a lot smaller than they currently are, so I had no idea where I was.

I realised, "Okay I am still alive, I can't walk, I was in a wheelchair, or sorry, in bed, immobilised." I had muscular neuropathy and what that means is if you don't use your muscles within 24 hours they deteriorate, so I had to walk again, I had to learn how to talk again – I had a trachea go down through my throat and I realised that I went through an episode with cancer, I realised I had this near death experience and the light. The purpose wasn't so clear to me until a good two to three years later, just serve and you will be, once again, shown that purpose. I kept on thinking, "It may be a big thing, I'm gonna be this, I'm gonna do that." But it wasn't.

I went back to work in the insurance field, I found myself talking more and more about my experience with the cancer to people, more than the insurance. I realised this was it because I didn't come out and say "Oh look, I had cancer." They all said to me "Oh, I know someone who has cancer," or their daughter or themselves, or there was a loved one near them that had cancer. So then I realised that my purpose was to tell them my story. Not to impress them but to impress upon them what is available, what can happen with the power of thought, with the power of manifestation, with the power of belief and the power of action to overcome these events.

The website came alongside with the realisation that I need to touch people out there, I need to get something out there to the world, not just to people that are in direct contact with me by either being in the business as an insurance broker or just

Michael's Thoughts on Miracles

every now and then. I need to get it out there more and more and more because people have got a need for this, people must be privilege to this information because it is a holistic approach, it's not just one thing as it is not just one thing that gave me the cancer, we use an holistic approach meaning the spiritual, the mental, the physical side and more appropriately, the mental side – the power of thought, I believe that 70% or 80% of my survival is just by the fact that I have a good mental attitude.

I believe that the body itself has its own healing power if we let it heal, and part of that power is innate in every one of us. Through the power of our thoughts, we can bring about this innate power. Be grateful for what you've got, not what you haven't got. Don't focus on the disease, focus on a wonderful life that you're going to enjoy, focus on that instead.

My health is fantastic. I have not, to this day, let down my guard in any area. As far as the physical goes, I still go to the gym, I still exercise regularly, be it walking or be it jogging, I keep a very positive mindset, read a lot of motivational material and I'm very grateful on a daily basis for all I have. Every morning I wake up and the first thing I do is say my prayer of gratefulness, be it for the little things, just the sunshine, just a bird singing, just a flower blooming, just the beauty of nature. If we don't stop and reflect on all that, we miss the whole purpose, we miss the whole point. It is a wonderful miracle in itself and the divine is unconditional, it's loving, it's caring, it's unconditional love that you feel and I guess a lot of people ask me "How do you know when a miracle has occurred for you?" Believe me, you know that fuzzy feeling, inside that warm feeling when you're in synchronicity – when you feel good, good thoughts project that feeling to you.

Another good example was when I had wanted to work for this company for a couple of years after I came out of the experience with the cancer. I was sitting there one day and wondering should I call this person, and about five minutes later, the phone rings and that person I was about to call calls me. And he says "Hey, what are you doing" and I said "You wouldn't believe this, I was just about to call you." So I guess that in itself is a miracle in the making. A lot of people will say that's just coincidence. But is it really? I mean, how many times have we had that same coincidence so to speak happen to us? We think "Oh god, you know I wish my mother, or my friend or my brother or whoever it may be would call me" and in that minute they do call you. So what had happened to me, that person did call me, we set up an appointment and I am now working quite happily with them in the company and have been for the last six years.

Another miracle is that we put together in our mind to build this mansion in the countryside. We actually saw this same mansion in our mind's eye before it ever manifested, we held that picture firmly imbedded in our mind at all stages. Now if someone had asked us five or six years ago "Do you ever think you could build this, go through the process of being an owner builder and the headaches and the hassles?" I would have said no. We just went on that gut feeling, we knew that a miracle was about to happen, we were guided by that powerful intervention that none of that negative stuff mattered. It was all just holding onto that visualisation believing firmly and experiencing it inside before it ever comes to fruition, that feeling was just an elated feeling that nothing stopped us from moving forward. Yes, there were some headaches, there were some setbacks but it didn't matter. At the end of it, we are living now in this beautiful mansion surrounded by beauty all around the countryside and it is the house of our dreams and that in itself, I believe, is a true miracle.

In the past, like I suppose most of us would do, I'd stop in my tracks and I'd say to myself "Oh god, why me, why is this

Michael's Thoughts on Miracles

happening?" Now I look back on it and say to myself "Well hang on a second, I can't afford to think like this, there must be some good out of this." Like the cancer, a lot of people would say to me "Poor you." No, you don't realise, but it's the best thing that's ever happened to me. It's the best thing because it's a big wakeup call. It's getting back to the perspective, the reality of life – we used to take it for granted before. Saying things to myself like "Oh, I'll do it tomorrow." Well, tomorrow never comes, it's always today, so now, you put things back into perspective. I do things today, I make the best out of my life. And I also now look at it on the basis that good can come out of anything. I look at it on the basis that "Ok, there is a lesson here, what can be good about this?" What can I do to improve the situation, what can I do to perhaps tell my story to someone else, to benefit someone else who may be going through the same conditions or hardships that I am?"

I am a strong believer in what we think, we manifest. I can't afford to stay too long in that negative state. And by also saying that, I don't mean that I'm going to stand up and all the time be happy. You can be sad at certain intervals in your life, it's only human nature. I prefer to be in a positive state; I put on some very nice music, read my favourite book or go out and enjoy the sunshine, walk the dog, just little things that count. As I said, I listen to music or pray, just take a couple of deep breaths and say to myself "This too shall pass", and it does.

Your stomach area is like your internal guidance system. You start to feel good inside. You start to feel happy for unknown reasons to you. Everything seems to be floating, everything seems to be in sync, everything seems to be so moving without any stoppage, without any disruptions, it just seems to be in a flow, a state. It's like you're being channelled. Sometimes, as the words are coming out of your mouth, you know yourself they're not your words. You're being touched by divine intervention. I believe that what we're doing in reality is going within, listening to that internal guidance within and you know that you are on track. You soon know the opposite too, when you're all knotted up, when your mind is cloudy, you don't want to be there too long. This is the correct definition of a miracle. It is from within, it is from the deeper space, embracing the universal love in silence, the unconditional love that is flowing through us. If only we allow it to flow and not stop it through our negative thoughts, or by our negative actions and ideas.

We can get back into the flow just by taking some time out. For example, by just putting on your favourite music. A lot of times it may be hard to do that because you may be in that state of flux. Accept it and just say to yourself 'this too shall pass'. Go away, reflect on what you're doing and put on some beautiful music, go for a walk, close your eyes and focus on your breathing, concentrating on the breath, read your favourite book or look at an image of something that inspires you. Or just phone a friend. Whatever it takes, just get into that nice state again, it's not that hard to do.

I truly believe that we have the power to make miracles happen in our life. It has been established that we are a spiritual being experiencing a physical body or a physical realm. And I believe that if we are part spirit and we have a soul, then why can't we manifest just like in the Bible, just like we've been taught through the spirit? Even in the Bible, it says 'ask and you shall be given'. It's by asking that it is given, but it's also the feeling associated with it, the belief, the gratitude and the power resides within feeling the vibration that makes the miracles happen. I truly believe that every one of us has the power to make miracles happen by our thoughts, by our feelings, by our attitudes, by the vibration being in sync.

Michael's Thoughts on Miracles

When I was in the coma, alongside the bed with me, there was a gentleman laying there who was given up on by the doctors. They were about to pull the machine on him. He was pronounced dead or being given up for dead. His son came in and fought with the doctors and said "No, how dare you, this is my father. I have got the power, and only I, to make the decision, or my family to make the decision to pull the machine." And they said "You don't understand son, your father's been given up for dead, he'll be a vegetable for life." The son fought hard and it was decided to give it another 24 hours, and I think it was the next day that that same man woke up from his death bed and was sitting up on the bed as if nothing had happened. So, to me, that is a miracle in the making.

I've seen many people like that in hospital visits. A good friend's mother was in a coma, pronounced dead, she'll never ever open her eyes again, and we'll have to pull the plug on her. I went to visit the mother with my friend and slowly said a prayer, in my own mind believing that this woman would open her eyes again, and she did. So yes, miracles are apparent all about us, all we have to do is observe. And it could be the smallest of things, it could be the bloom of a flower, it could be the smile of a child, it could be just the wonderful funny fuzzy feelings inside that we get when we appreciate the beauty of nature or the beauty of something that takes our eye.

Miracles start to happen in our life if we truly have a meaningful specific thing that we want to manifest. Put the thought out there, feel good inside, feel as though it's already happened, and don't just say things like 'I want more money.' Say things like "What will that money do for me?" Pretend it's already happened. Pretend that you're experiencing that. Don't doubt it. Release it to the universe. Know fully that it will manifest. It may not happen overnight, but it will happen. The universe will put you in touch with the people, with events that will lead you to the manifestation of what you are after. Be it health, be it money, be it relationships, whatever it is, it will happen, provided that you keep up the good feeling. As I said, pretend that it's already happened and align yourself, align the vibration which must be in harmony with what you ask for. Watch the miracles start to flow to you.

> "A miracle is an event which creates faith. That is the purpose and nature of miracles. Frauds deceive. An event which creates faith does not deceive and therefore is not a fraud, but a miracle." – George Bernard Shaw

Michael's Thoughts on Miracles

C - Centering –
Become the Captain of Your Soul

C - CENTERING – BECOME THE CAPTAIN OF YOUR SOUL

C - Centering – Become the Captain of Your Soul

We are often told to centre, to focus, to find our peace. In fact, people have been trying to do this for a very long time; from Monks, who became hermits in caves, to people who attend retreats to find their place and their peace in this world. We are all trying to find our centre. As part of the odyssey trip that accompanied the writing of this book, I had the very great joy of finding myself walking around the standing stones at Stonehenge near Salisbury in England. Now these standing stones have attracted many theories over the years and I am not going to add another one. I mention them because as I

C – Centering – Become the Captain of Your Soul

wandered around their perimeter, I tried to imagine what it was like to see them being built, to participate in their building and planning and as I did this I gazed upon their centre point. The standing stones, the act of walking in a circle had made me very reflective yet at the same time very focused. This action made me remember something that I had read about Charles Darwin. At his home on the outskirts of England he had a walking garden. Darwin's 'sand-walk', or 'thinking path', was created in 1846 when a 0.6ha area of land was fenced off and planted out with native trees and a circular path dressed with sandy gravel around the edge. Darwin would take his daily constitutional and walk a number of times around the sand-walk counting the laps with flints piled at the beginning of the circuit. It was strolling around this path where he did most of his thinking. http://www.english-heritage.org.uk

Creating a circular path was important to Darwin to enable him to do his thinking. He surrounded himself with nature and pondered on the questions and the things that he observed. Carl Jung took to drawing Mandalas for himself and for his patients. He observed what the circle contained. He pondered on the contents of the drawings and saw them as a way that the centre point of the individual was trying to communicate. So, if we look at these few examples, we can begin to see that focus and then letting go are really important facets of bringing us to our centre. Whatever means an individual devises to do this, through meditation, prayer, walking, retreating, painting, drawing mandalas; the more one is able to do it, the more one can find that peace in an instant when things are not quite going according to plan and to ensure that those miracles keep flooding our life.

"Smooth sailing never made a skillful sailor." – Earl Nightingale

Whilst for the most part, we live in the hope that everything will be good all the time, there are often challenges along the way. Being able to activate that centre point, that focus, then allows us to reconnect to the infinite intelligence, our communion with God. Here we are able to find the strength to continue, the answers to guide us and the courage to keep stepping. Rather, challenges can be viewed as a means to pull in, pull back and reconnect. By doing this, we then find the resilience to keep moving forward in life.

> "Courage is not simply one of the virtues, but the form of every virtue at the testing point." - C.S. Lewis

For that courage comes to us through the path of infinite intelligence. Trusting in this with all our faith is the best way to find the means to overcome whatever obstacle may stand in your way. Our belief that this is there for us comes from our centre, from our divine spark. Connecting to this on a daily basis is really like having a preplanned route that gets you to work quicker. The more you use it, the more it becomes second nature. At our centre we find stillness, we find space, we find peace and we find answers and directions when none seem apparent. You might now be thinking "well that's fine, but what does it really mean". It means that we can find the space in our lives to create our own world.

We can participate fully in the tasks around us and the daily living. We can participate fully as we have a clear centre and clear focus, we focus on the now; as yesterday and tomorrow have no impact. The point of focus when heart and mind are in communion brings us our centre; it is the charge to our divine

C – Centering – Become the Captain of Your Soul

nature. It does not mean that we retreat from all things it means rather that we have a knowing that we can achieve everything and we can find the path that will accommodate us in our journey. It also means that we connect to others by passing on some of the things that we have been given. This may be through giving of our time, our money, and our ideas to help others progress. In a sense, part of the crediting to our miracle bank account is in paying forward to others so that they in turn begin to see the possibilities in their own lives. We can empower others just through sharing our story with them, as really being involved with those around us is important to our centre as well. For when we have clearly defined our centre, we do not let others impact on us, but rather we impact on the world in a positive and productive way.

If we watch children play or investigate the tiniest spec of dirt on their shoe, we begin to remember that sense of wonder and joy we all used to find in simple things. Returning to that mindset helps us to recognise those small everyday miracles that are there just waiting to be acknowledged. How often have you asked for that car space in your head when you have been running late and there it is? "A coincidence" you say, and park the car and rush to the next appointment. How often have you been jogging and gone past the point of heat exhaustion and then suddenly from nowhere a gentle breeze comes at your beckoning and offers you cooling? Again a coincidence, or perhaps another way of looking at the small miracles that come at our beckoning. If we view these with the childlike wonder of our earlier days, then we can again become inspired as to the endless possibilities that abound in our life. We begin to see that we are able to create our world and enjoy our connection with everyone around us. Think back to your childhood and remember a time when you would be creative. It may have been drawing, it may have been singing, it may have been your imaginary friend. What feeling did you have then? Can you bring that feeling back into your life?

I believe that you can, and finding your centre is a great way to bring the sense of wonder back to your everyday world. For we have a choice how we react to things and miracles are no different. We can see them as just a pleasant coincidence or we can thank them and see them as a small blessing in our day. We have the choice to acknowledge and gather a sense of wonder around the events that take place in our daily living. We can see them as either fantastic things and harness that childlike joy again, or we can merely wander through our day as if life is drained of those small things that as children we rejoiced in. My vote is for the childlike joy and that is my choice, as you will make one also. In fact, we have that time in our thinking that allows us to make the choice. Even if we are surprised with events, we can choose our reaction to them and miracles are no different. If we react to a miracle in a positive way, then there is a good chance that we will find another one in our day as well. The more we acknowledge them, both big and small, the more we will find them in our day. Good thoughts attract good things and when we focus on the good things in our lives, we find that we are overwhelmed with what we have and that in turn reminds us of our miraculous nature and the wonderful world in which we live.

> *"Synchronicity is an ever present reality for those who have eyes to see."*
>
> Carl Jung

C – Centering – Become the Captain of Your Soul

"Miracles or coincidences", the title of the book, comes from the two viewpoints that people give the synchronicity or happenstances in their lives. If you choose to believe that miracles do exist, then you live in that world. You do not have to convince anyone else of their occurrence or what they may mean to you. Again, it comes down to choice and your choice may differ from someone else's. By all means, if you want to share your experiences with others, please do so, but know that's not required. Allow yourself the wonder of what might happen in your life and allow that to be enough confirmation that miracles do exist. There will always be people who have a different view, but don't let that take away from your own wonder around events. For me, even getting to the point of writing this book has been a miraculous odyssey. Things and people have flowed to me and offered their support and time without the demand of recompense. People have offered their own stories and I have heard many wonderful stories of miraculous healings, of events, of the small things that people are grateful for in their lives. I have been amazed that people receive my ideas with such generosity of spirit and encouragement.

The kindness of these people only enhances the confirmation for me that writing this book is the correct thing. In fact, people have been so willing to share their experiences that it is like there is room for not one book, but many more books, to recount all the events that people have experienced in their lives. The flow of wanting to write the book, and in being open to the things that people offer, has in fact led to the book almost creating itself. Yes, I am typing the draft that you are ultimately reading, but the contents are not mine alone. The slipstream of events has allowed for stories and people to show themselves and be included in these pages. I have taken action to write to people and ask for their thoughts, I have taken action to talk to people about the book, but beyond that the flow greets me to assist with places and events. Carl Jung, a psychiatrist around the time of Sigmund Freud, did much work around the collective unconscious; that greater part of the whole from which ideas flow amongst cultures, countries, the past and to the future. It gives us those moments when we feel like we have a shared knowledge and it leaves an indelible sense of place in us that is inexplicable.

"As far as we can discern, the sole purpose of human existence is to kindle a light in the darkness of mere being." Carl Jung

C – Centering – Become the Captain of Your Soul

Sometimes we are given clues about our lives and about the miracles that come to us. When we openly acknowledge those small things, they sometimes are the prelude to bigger things. When on the odyssey journey of the cruise ship, my husband and I had booked to go to a region in France for a day trip. The trip was overbooked and a small group of us went to Mont Saint Michel instead. The cruise director told me that it was the place that they believed J K Rowling had modelled her image of Hogwarts. To someone who was contemplating writing a book, this seemed like a wonderful "coincidence". Yes it was, this place was one of the most dramatic experiences of the trip. A wonderful monastery was built on a rocky outcrop surrounded by quicksand. The dream had come about through one man's vision of Archangel Michael many hundreds of years ago. The abbey had gone through change and had been the subject of attack many times, but it survived and its sovereignty was never lost.

Atop this wonderful outcrop stands a golden statue of Michael. Walking through the corridors of the past and into the cloisters of the abbey I was spellbound. My childlike wonder returned to me and the error of an overbooking brought a miracle of awareness. For the story of one man's vision still stands today, albeit altered and changed many times, but with no less feeling that it had before. To me this symbolised acceptance that we can make our lives truly miraculous and pass this on for others.

We have the ability to be the Captains of our Soul, and to achieve our dreams. Our dreams may be big or small, but they can be achieved. Our sense of wonder and the realm of possibility drive us beyond the limitations of our current existence. We may not all have the vision, the clue to build something like Mont Saint Michel, but isn't it wonderful just knowing that someone else did. Our direction has a co pilot and we can walk with our divine spark and facilitate these things in our life. God, or infinite intelligence, is just waiting for us to ask. It is important to express our desires clearly and for us to acknowledge those clues along the way that lead us ever closer to our desires. For the action towards our goals brings about the miracles that help us complete them.

Knowing our centre helps us meet our co-pilot and we can achieve beyond our previous successes. In fact, if we watch what others have done, seek out coaches who can bring us guidance to help us find our own way, then we are really enhancing not detracting from our own abilities. We are taking the action required to take us to new levels. We are the Captain of our Soul and just sometimes we need extra crew to navigate our way.

As I spoke about before, we are able to set pathways that bring us into the flow and through acknowledging our centre and working from that place we are given a clarity that allows us to find our way to our dreams, goals and visions. Our centre

C – Centering – Become the Captain of Your Soul

connects us, our centre is the balance of our hearts and minds – a bit like love and marriage, you can't have one without the other. Seeking assistance to find our centre is not a weakness, it is rather a way of expediting our learning. We can all learn to paint, but if we follow someone who is already painting, we find ways to reach our finished product that much quicker.

One last thing on Mont Saint Michel, in the cloisters where past priests, monks and others have gathered to find their centre, there was a small indentation worn into the seat. I wonder how many or how much time had been spent in finding illumination in that place? For that heritage still exists for future generations to view and wonder and journey to their centre.

ACTION STEPS:

1. Acknowledge all the small things that help your day.
2. Take the time to connect to your centre; find the ways that work for you.
3. Observe events around you and connect their meaning to you.
4. When challenged, return to the centre and navigate from there.

"To leave the circumference for the centre is equivalent to moving from the exterior to the interior, from form to contemplation, from multiplicity to unity, from space to spacelessness, from time to timelessness. In all symbols expressive of the mystic Centre the intention is to reveal to Man the meaning of the primordial 'paradisal state' and to teach him to identify himself with the supreme principle of the universe." Cirlot

C – Centering – Become the Captain of Your Soul

Kerrianne Cox's Thoughts on Miracles

KERRIANNE COX'S THOUGHTS ON MIRACLES

Kerrianne Cox is an elder of Beagle Bay in the Kimberleys and is a successful performer in her own right. She sings from the heart of our land. Kerrieanne is an indigenous woman and out of respect for her culture and story I have left this interview in its powerful raw form to avoid placing an incorrect interpretation on her words.

I first met Kerrianne when she performed at the Blue Mountains Blues festival several years ago. Kerrianne held the audience captivated as she called in the people of the land. A mist rolled into the big tent, which brought the ancestors to welcome us to the place. Kerrianne continues to inspire and enrich us through her performances and her life. I was privileged to talk with Kerrianne about miracles and the wonderful world in which we live. Please read on and share Kerrianne's magical journey. Story and place are important to us all and if we listen, we learn and open our hearts to new horizons.

The gas business Kerrianne talks about is the decision by the Western Australian government to do exploratory searches for gas in the Kimberley, one of the most beautiful wilderness places in our country and the world.

Kerrieanne: I've just been dealing with the gas business up there.

Geraldine: How's that going?

Kerrieanne: It's kind of - it's pretty hard when you have to deal with your own people who are subject to struggles still, so the easy way out is always the best approach for people who have lived in that type of life, you know?

Geraldine: They don't want to hassle. They just give in easily?

Kerrieanne: Yeah, and I think because of the government control over us for such a long time. It's spread into a lot of our people's mentality to just subject themselves to dictatorship. They support the government's bully tactics and corporate mining companies to do the same in that sense. Money talks, but money, that type of money, I don't believe will do any kind of good in the long term. At the same time, the country gets stuffed up and you get an influx of people who are not linked in the country; they're more part of the mining kind of world and destruction of country and so their interests are very different.

Geraldine: Do you think you'll be able to sort of turn the tide and hang on?

Kerrieanne: Yeah, I'm hanging on. We're not there saying well, it's all over. We have faith in ourselves and in the country.

Geraldine: Truth will win out too.

Kerrieanne: That's right. I'm working with my mum, you know, to work up where her mum and grannies come from. Since about six months ago, we just found out that our grannies were part of that- that was their country where the proposed gas plant is going to be and it's just a bit heartbreaking. We've been searching all our lives and working out who we are and where we come from, and then we find out finally where we come from and then it's this big challenge in front of us, you know?

Geraldine: Maybe it's just the right timing. It's almost like the gift from the ancestors to help save it.

Kerrianne goes on to tell us about contact she had with her long dead ancestors but she could not go on to write about it herself. Australian Aboriginal avoidance practices require that, for example, Aborigines not discuss or write about death or, with today's technology, watch television programmes which contain content about death. Or certain people were required to avoid others in their family or clan in traditional Aboriginal society. These avoidance practices are a mark of respect and these customs are still active in many parts of Australia, to a greater or lesser extent.

Kerrieanne: Yes, definitely. I don't worry. I talked to that woman my grandmother from that country. She'd come and light up the full moon, you know? Three years it was before one of my nephews was born. He was born on the ninth of October and the full moon was the week before that and the women channeled themselves through my cousin, Anna. It was quite freaky at first. We talked about all this stuff. The land stuff and everything, but I didn't quite understand it then. I'm conscious of the link of what the women were trying to tell me at that time through her. It was an amazing experience and I think Anna kind of stayed away from me for a long time after that. She was just like, I don't know what's happening to my body and this is just too freaky K, and I just said "that's your gift. You have a pure heart and they can talk through you and they've chosen you to talk through."

Geraldine: How did she settle after that? Did it take her quite a long time?

Kerrieanne: Yeah. She never came around for like five or six months. What happened is I started to see a change in Anna- like they've been telling me she's actually in a waiting room- a waiting dimension in her spirit. They've taken over and told me to apologize to Anna for using her body that way. It was my grandmother- my dead grandmother- that I've never met.

Geraldine: Wow and she came through that way?

Kerrieanne: Yeah, and it was an honor from the Earth. From Rock of Ages. She said I've been waiting for this for a long time my baby. Here I am to talk to you for the country. We're giving you that. Me and my sister cried because we knew it was her. We went and got a photo of her as she died when my mum was 16 so when we saw her we were beside ourselves.

Geraldine: Wow. Such an amazing thing to happen. Hard to fathom.

Kerrieanne: Certainly and I said, "How are you able to do this? To form yourself?" She said, "well, we women of the moon are able to form through the luminescence of the light of the moon on full."

Geraldine: And that's how they can do it?

Kerrieanne: Yeah and she came through. She's in this manifestation of material form. She was given that honor from the spirit, you know? To come and talk to me and she got me prepared and she asked me whether I wanted to take this responsibility on that was a gift and a curse. I said that I'd be very honored. I had been waiting for it in some way. I knew in my being that this is what I had to do and the next thing another woman- an old woman- came through. Rock of Ages. Very, very amazing, you know? It was like an initiation kind of ceremony and Anna and I are right now because we talk about it and I said, "Anna, they were telling us and where they want to have that gas plant is where my grandmother's rock is." There's a woman in the shape of a rock with a dog. I've been looking and searching for this rock as it's a sacred place. I've been searching for her for four years. Looking in the wrong country.

Geraldine: And you found her?

Kerrieanne: And I found her. I haven't been there yet, but I found her through- what had happened is when my grandmother had said six generations of bones in that cave and then there are six generations of us since we've been taken off of the land. I'm fifth generation to my great, great, great grandmother, of the Ngumbarl women .She was taken off the land by the wealthy and she was sent to the Claremont mad house, as well as Rosie, her daughter, which is my mother's mother and that's when the in laws took over the laws of that country and they've been holding it for 80 years. They're the Nyikina who are fighting to stop the gas in the country, but they kept a lot of stuff from us as well. It's really interesting how the gas has brought them to working with us and they now can't deny our place and they need to tell us our dreaming and all that stuff.

Geraldine: That's really opened up a whole range of things.

Kerrieanne: Yeah and I have this on my chest because I was getting a lit bit frustrated and angry at the men from Goolarboloo people who are Nyikina because they've been holding the law for 80 years and I said, my mother hasn't been recognized in that place where the country needs her and the people need her to lead now with me. I spoke to him the other day. Something kind of happened where they want to kick us out of the negotiations and I spoke to him and I said, it's not really about the people and we just found out that we are Ngumbarl women and our grandmothers were taken off the land I explained to him that's how he came into the picture because he was a Nyikina man and our great grandfather was a Nyikina man and we're taking our place now. I felt really good. It was really funny that everything just lifted from me after I had spoken to him.

Geraldine: You just had to get it off your chest and clear it.

Kerrianne Cox's Thoughts on Miracles

Kerrieanne: Yeah. It felt really good. He didn't argue with me. He agreed with me and that was the first time that he had to be honest and true about the truth. I felt really strong about it and saying so, and now he needs us more than ever.

Geraldine: Isn't that wonderful? That sort of almost brings about the clans going again to support each other rather than argue about who has control.

Kerrieanne: Certainly. We're good people. We will respect a rightful place for them so they have a place there.

Geraldine: And to work together.

Kerrieanne: We clearly have to start now and between us and his clan who has been there for 80 years- his grandfather said that one day the rightful people will come back and we have to give them back the law and culture and we're back now, you know?

Geraldine: So he knew.

Kerrieanne: Yeah and he doesn't know how to do that because we women have our Law too and we have to find a way forward with the men who have been running it. That was my frustration because I already had been in contact with the land. The land spoke to me. My grandmother was a symbol of the land of Ngumbarl clan, you know? It's just amazing. It's going to be an interesting time and also, it's going to make me more powerful in my own self now because I know who I am now, you know? I know where my father is but I've always yearned to know where grandmother was and now I know where she is, you know?

Geraldine: Isn't that great?

Kerrieanne: And that's where we all are - my mum, me, my sisters, and we can return and become empowered because we found an omen. We were violated off our land. My grandmothers were raped of course and they contracted syphilis and syphilis goes to the head and that was the main reason of course why they were sent to Claremont.

Geraldine: Yeah, I was going to ask how that happened, but now I understand.

Kerrieanne: Yeah. That's the proper way. In the native welfare report where we found a document last year on my auntie's table and we just took it because they had been holding information from us. It said that Rosie Bobby /Kelly was taken off the land because she spoke Ngumbarl and was sent to the madhouse. She is buried in Fremantle Cemetery in Perth. So we know where they are now and we can bring them home, you know? Yeah, Kimberley law and culture- they're responsible for those things now for bringing remains back of people. We have lots of support to let us move through the system.

So it's just really funny. Through my partner, who worked with Family Prevention legal service- she went there for a conference and this woman was one of the coordinators in the other units and Rose just felt she had dementia and mentioned her name and she said, oh, I know that name. She started to talk about the story and···

Geraldine: So they're miracles, yeah.

Kerrieanne: Yeah, they are. You know what I'm telling you? It's pretty much relevant to your book.

Geraldine: Yeah, it is. It ties in miracles happening in that spirit and how that comes to you, but also how it's helping you to fight the battle to protect the land, which is relevant to all of us in the world. To protect that sacred land. Land is sacred to us.

Kerrianne Cox's Thoughts on Miracles

Kerrieanne: Certainly, certainly. What happens here happens everywhere, you know? We're part of the same matrix and stuff. It's starting to- the time is right now, you know? I was quite anxious and I believe people who are a bit ahead of their time- which I was back then- I had to learn how to be patient with everything. With the changes. I really feel like now the universe is really opening up now and the evolution on the planet is starting to progress. It's shifting because I've been trying to get the model concept up of sustainability and conserving and empowering Aboriginal Australia because they need to play a really vital part with the knowledge base. The connection to country for everybody to return is really important because we don't really have much time. The reality is that some of us- a lot of us- will move through wherever we are and go and those who choose to will be left behind. Because of Earth calling and she's alive, you know? I'm just a power talk.

Geraldine: Yeah, that's it. You're providing a means for her to express.

Kerrieanne: To express and she speaks whenever she does. I know when she's moving through me, you know? So that night was really important and that was a really sacred night. It was a ceremony that was done on the full moon and we didn't know. We were guided by the spirit and the women came. It was such an amazing moment. My sister was there, my young sister and she's my right hand man, eh?

Geraldine: Yeah. Is it something like a tradition handed down that you knew what to do? Or was it something that you really felt compelled to do on that night?

Kerrieanne: I felt that it was right and I didn't question 'why me' because in my journey if I can kind of reflect back on my childhood and growing up I always yearned to be spiritually

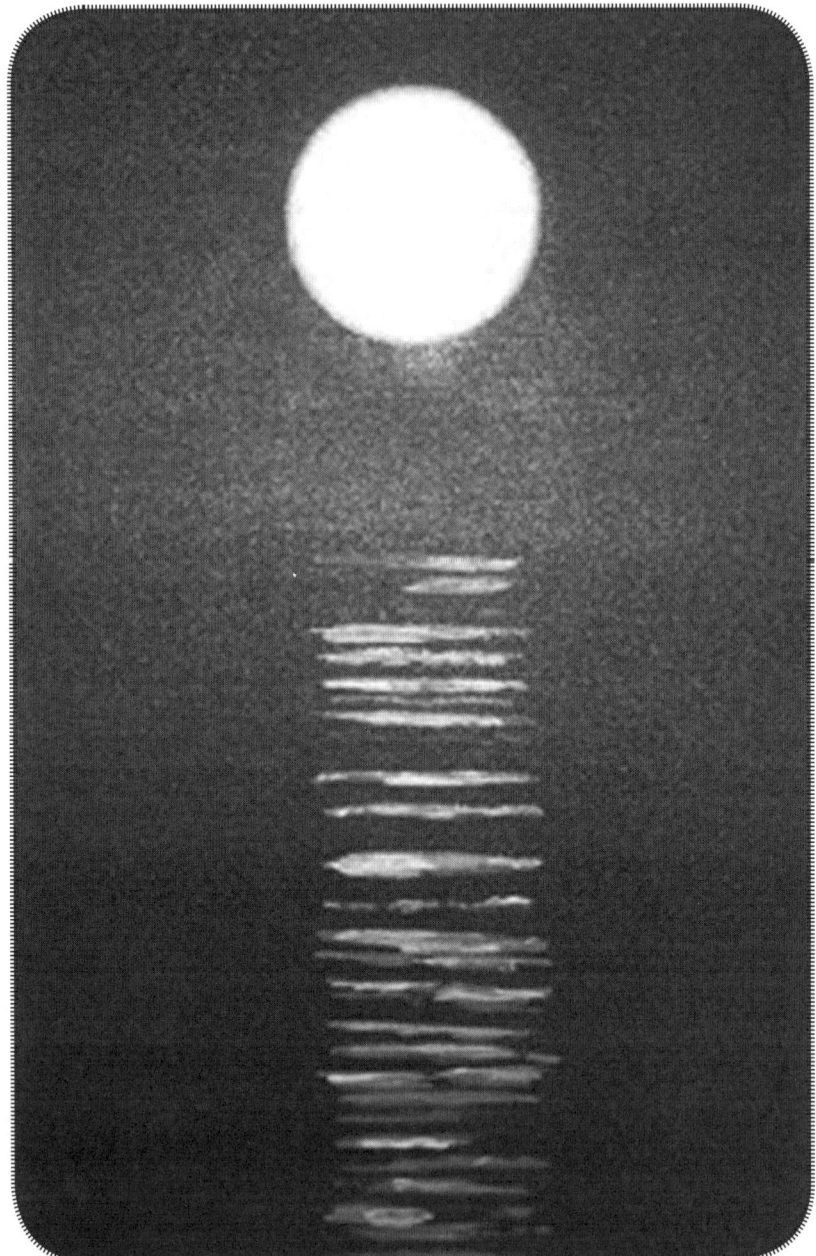

Painting by Kaylene Gayner

Kerrianne Cox's Thoughts on Miracles

enlightened and to have a greater understanding of Earth and the universe and everything and how we're all connected. Through my hard work and through my own healing and growth, I was rewarded. One of the things they told me was the fact that they looked at all their children. I don't like to talk much about this because some people- they looked at all the children on Earth and they said that they saw me and that I never forgot them. I always talked about them and I always stayed connected with them. That was my music and my message. So they basically honored me by the four directions of the Earth. They honored me and gave me the language of the Earth- from the four corners of the Earth and that language is the heart. Not what we speak now, but- through that when they said it was a curse and gift; it's a fact that I was given a gift. I was given a direct connection from Heaven and Earth. We're all a part of Heaven and Earth. I can see you and I can see people and I can see where they're hurting. I can see where they're needing healing and stuff. It was a preparation if I go back to the time when I was in South Africa, where I met a very powerful being. He was a very evolved being who meditated in crystals and he broke the encodes. He's a father and he said to me that it was wrong of him to- that the father should take the full responsibility of the Earth and that he couldn't do it and he realized that and that he needed the mother to create a balance. He said through that, in order for me to heal, the mother needs to heal now. As women, as a representative of Earth, we need to heal in order for the men to heal and then the Sun will heal too. When I met him I wanted to run away because he- I knew who he was and he saw that through me and I saw right through him. I knew I was going to meet him and he conjures me. He gave me the tools and he brought me back to the Earth, eh? I went right into the ground and I cried for the first time. I was really sorry that I had not been there for a long time, you know?

Geraldine: Not been present⋯

Kerrieanne: Yeah. The last thing he said to me was really interesting. He said, "I've broke all the encodes" of the program. The cellular- within our cells, that's where the program is- the cycle, you know? He said that he was able to break through because he dealt with his father and he helped to heal his mother and he recognized her in her true light of who she was and he prepared- he got his father and he was up on the big story building and he was prepared to jump for him to take him out for what he was doing to his mother. He was shock treating her. Putting his mother in shock constantly and within that moment that he jumped from the building, his father had a heart attack and he was given life for making a sacrifice, you know? It's not how you take it literally. It's the meaning.

Geraldine: It's the meaning.

Kerrieanne: Yeah, in that sense. He did say to me that he didn't know what woman's place was on the planet.

Geraldine: Until he met you and then he⋯

Kerrieanne: Yeah. I knew. It's what you call woman's business because the reality is in order for man's law to sustain itself and have life on the planet, woman's law must be the first to activate it, eh? That's when I went to the bush last year in June. I went to my first woman's law camp and we practiced the rituals of the first woman on Earth. It goes back to the link of that ritual to man's business where young men-boys- become men, eh? They go through the initiation so it starts with us in that sense. Through that, everything has kind of followed shape and form and I live my life through moments. I don't really know what is going to happen tomorrow, but all I can do is dream tomorrow for what I want so I have to be very clear on what I want tomorrow to be if it's given to me. Just to read the signs that are happening constantly around you and to walk in part⋯

Geraldine: You see it at a different level from most of us in that you sort of see the spiritual level of life as well?

Kerrieanne: Yeah, the spirits are talking to me. E- E is not he or she- that's what we say at home. E went over there because there's no gender in our culture. Never has been. It's like today. See, one of the things I have to do- I have to give up smoking and it's been quite interesting because I know I have to do that now because it's time. E is telling me it's time Kerrieanne, you know? It's been really interesting because the places that I've stayed at I've had to walk up these big hills and stuff and I'm going, alright, I get it.

Kerrieanne: And I'm going, you got me. I'm with you. Yep, yep, yep. But I've been- my partner and I have been planning on a date and we're getting a bit of support through the doctors to help me and my partner. It was just really interesting that this is just confirming it's time. I've been reading it. I've been reading the signs. I've been hearing her talk, you know? Yeah, it's really good. Even with my meetings. I have a meeting with the Westpac Foundation because I've adopted a model that's come through my own spiritual healing and transformation that I want to kind of adapt in different places. I've had quite a lot of successful meetings within corporate Australia and the philanthropy and non for profit sectors. I went to see this Westpac woman and she helped me to understand what type of structure I needed to create to be able to house these different arms to be able to have the support and resources to be able to roll out the model on the ground. It's a model that supports- that works with individuals who are ready to take that journey. They're supported for two years in Aboriginal communities. Anybody being able to just move in and I've been waiting for backing for almost four years now and it hasn't happened, but it's happening now. It's just funny because that old spirit again has been saying, look, it's time, okay, you know? It's all happening. As I was walking down the streets of Sydney to find Kent Street- there was these people and they were just so helpful, you know? To me, they are like angels helping me along to say, you've got to get to this meeting and made sure that I found Kent Street and that I found Westpac Foundation and I think that old spirit again- I say thank you for your blessing. I'm on the right track. I'm meant to be doing this. This is right. I'm doing well. That's been kind of- the science again in that sense. Those little stories and stuff because for awhile- the last year it's been really hard just trying to work out whether it was right or not. It was kind of bringing me down a little bit because you have to be patient in that sense, but I knew that I needed to kind of clear a lot of stuff in my life? Since I've been doing that and the meeting with the grandmothers and the law business and the gas stuff, it's just boiled to a head. I think I've grown too and moved higher up the mountain. From that it's created a shift on the macro level that's opened up the doorways now for all these opportunities that are happening. All those kinds of things are starting to shape themselves on that level and that's all I really know?

Geraldine: In the book I describe it as being lifted into a slipstream. It's sort of the flow then helps you into the direction you are wanting to go. You talk about it like dreaming tomorrow. It's the same thing. You put clearly what you want the day to be like, rather than to have the day subjected on you.

Kerrieanne: That's right. That's right. And being able to stay positive is really important because as you lay down for the night- whatever your thoughts are, you know? If it's positive it supports that reality to take shape.

Geraldine: With having that sense- you talk about it being like a gift and a curse, does it sometimes frighten you to have that huge responsibility that is coming with that spirit connection?

Kerrieanne: It does because I work really hard and there are a lot of people who come to me constantly. I'm working and when you're healing, you're taking a lot of their stuff in and you're having to work hard to release that too in that sense. I can see people- I can see them really clearly like the people- I've got a reputation for being a mind reader. This is really freaky, Kerrieanne. You can read our thoughts. And I'm like, no, it's like I'm inside of you and you're inside of me and we are one. Because I'm sitting in that place, I'm showing you how to come there too, you know? Because we are the same. When I heal you, then you heal me and you'll heal it just as well as I am. It's constant. It's constant. Everywhere I go. Sometimes I can't walk down the street, you know? When it's full on.

Geraldine: Do you struggle with that? Since you pick up so much from other people?

Kerrieanne: I do and this is where- this is my next part where I have to shape myself. My health, my dietary needs, nutrition, all that stuff. Leaving my addictions- whatever they are- even coffee in that sense and being really clear and also being able to support the dream of being able to build a sanctuary out in country where I'm able to go back and have some retreat time for myself and recharge and all that. It does get really full on and I know that at some stage I really need to have support when I'm traveling. Just to help me with myself basically. I just get right into it and I forget about myself, you know? I'm constantly giving because we don't have a lot of time, so when I'm there, I'm going to do it. I deal with humbug people. I know when people have an agenda and they're wanting knowledge and all they want is just to gain and be greedy and take, take, take, take, take and I don't- I stop those types of people, you know? You can see them- I know when genuine people come and want to go through that shift and stuff and I'm there to support them through it. Just enlighten them to see it for what it truly is so they don't get caught up with the madness in that sense. At some stage, as it continues to get full on, to have support is really good. I had a friend who was with me in Port Fairy and she was really, really good. She would say like, alright Kerrieanne, let's take a break. Let's go out. Even if we have to sit in the car for half an hour for you to just center and chill for a little while because she knows I'm just working it. I'm working the crowd. I'm working the people. It's not what I'm saying. It's what I'm transmitting to them on a vibration, you know? On the energy frequency vibration and that's how we transmit stuff, you know? It's like radio. It's the same thing. Send and receive constantly.

Geraldine: Constantly.

Kerrieanne: Yeah and I was pushed to the brink two years ago when I went out there and had a whole week with the women and the children and I'm not only just trying to encourage and motivate and seeing their spirits to life and give them life and at the same time hold the energy in the communities to kind of keep the negativity out. So you're not just doing that. You're having to shield them too, you know? From the forces that are trying to challenge the light. Whether they're men- the type that try to keep women down. Whether its parents who are constantly neglecting their kids or whatever. It's that whole I'm able to protect that space and give them a safe environment while I'm there to be able to do my work, you know? It was constant for a week. I was quite sick when I got back. It totally took it out of me.

Geraldine: And how do you recharge after that? Is it just finding your space and being able to return to country and grounding and finding your spirit to renew?

Kerrieanne: That's right. That's right. Just being able to take myself out of everyone, you know? And be in the greenery. Be in the space or whatever opportunity I can do it, you know? Just to kind of disappear into the bush. Whether it's golf on the TV- I'll just disappear into the green, you know? Just to kind of relax and replenish myself. It's like going into that celestial park you know. You just nourish and bathe and cleanse yourself over and over again and stuff.

Geraldine: Because you are a performer, does music help you do that when you're not performing or because it's part of your toolkit, it's not as great a release for you?

Kerrieanne: It's a great friend, my music. It's been my life savior as well. It's been my strength and my tool to help me to where I've come at this stage. It's a very strong medium for me to use when I'm doing my work. People don't get so defensive about music in that sense, rather than if you're talking directly at them. Being a politician and speaking that talk. I think music has always been the universal way for all of us for a long time. It will always be in my life. It also helps me to- I don't think escape. It just helps me to relax and to go back to that place of truth and that place of light. Keeps all that negativity away, you know?

Geraldine: We've talked about it and for me; I've used the word miracle in the book. You talk about spirit and the things that happen- the little things that happen- along the way to show you that spirit is guiding. The spirit is saying you're on the right path. How would you describe those little things? Are they miracles or have you got a better description that you give to them?

Kerrieanne: Well, I think, yeah. We can call it miracle. I think it's just- you know when you're kind of- when you're a part of the universe and you know you're not just one in isolation. You are part of something greater and when those times happen- I know that I am working in unison with the universe. With Heaven and Earth in that sense. A lot of people- they are alone- until they realize they're not alone. They're part of this great big divine force, you know? That force that circulates within us, within the Earth, within the trees, within everything. I think I'm reminded of that constantly. People can say magic as well, but it's a sacred force that you're in touch with because you're part of the light. When I'm meditating, I can go within myself and that's who I am. I'm the light and I'm a part of a greater light, you know? When I tap into that, that's when you're part of a powerful or greater force and you're able to utilize it in a beautiful way and a positive way that affects people properly. That's why when you're ready, you're chosen because that's very powerful stuff. It can be destructive for people who don't know how to use it wisely.

Geraldine: Keeping a handle on that for people when they experience- what would you say is the best thing for someone to maintain that light and work with it as best they can?

Kerrieanne: This is where the calming approach comes in when you're just able to bring a sense of calmness and nurturing and through that you're able to bring them to that place of truth and the place of peace, eh? Where there's no worry. Where your problems start to disappear in that sense. I constantly use myself in part of my journey, you know? To confirm what they're moving through. I, too, have come from that place, but here I am. This is where I'm entering now, you know? And this is where you're moving. I never allow myself to be even higher than them, you know? But equal. Because people are vulnerable in that state and you can crush them and you can do anything so- they entrust that space to you and I'm to respect it in the most honored way for them to continue on the journey. It's knowing. I just know what they need because I'm them and they're me, you know? They're talking to me so when we're one, it's like their higher self is telling me what they require and all I'm doing is confirming what they already know. I tell them. Come on, let's not fool around. You exactly know what I'm talking about and don't be frightened, you know? Let's move to the next place now, you know? To the next level.

Geraldine: Do people, for the most part, understand if they find their way to you, does that mean that they are at a level where they're beginning to understand?

Kerrieanne: Yeah, they're ready. I know people who will stay in the background. They're not ready. They're still in their fear, you know? Others will come and just get their honey and be given a seed, you know? The seed of life. The seed to grow within them. To blossom and a guy, when I was at the Blue Mountains two years ago, he was crying and he came up to me and he said to me, "you know, Kerrieanne - I just really, really feel strongly that you came for me, you know? What you gave me was really amazing. I was filled with this amazing light and I feel full and I have a spirit and it's like you gave me a seed of life, you know? To grow." I said, "you know what brother? I want to thank you because you came. You received and how amazing you are to be able to do that for yourself and you should be thanking yourself for this day. I'm just here to support you on that journey and to light you up even more, you know, in that sense. It's you who you should thank in that sense. Not me."

Geraldine: It's amazing.

Kerrieanne: Because it's not really about me, you know? Geraldine? It's about them and I have to give them their power and for me to say, oh yeah, thanks a lot. Like yeah, I was pretty cool. That's ego, you know? Move away from the ego and I want to recognize and honor him because he's worked so hard to reach that stage where he has allowed that holy spirit to enter inside of him, you know? To be filled by that sacred force, by that Holy Spirit and to share that with me. I felt so honored and blessed to be a part of that moment and to embrace him and to acknowledge him for being truly open and for stepping forward and giving him a pat on the back and saying, "you're doing great and I'm so proud of you, you know? I'm so proud of you."

Geraldine: For him to have that experience and to want to speak with you about it and for you to be almost like the catalyst for him to be able to express it and to connect, you talk about ego and stepping back away from the ego. For him, as an example, how does he step beyond having that seed and moving with it?

Kerrieanne: Well, I think that my dreaming for him is only positive, eh? When I left that man in the room I knew that he was on to great stuff- greater things in his life. That he would- he was functioning better as a much more beautiful and whole human being. Wherever he went, he would give light to the people and places around him. That's all I know. That's all I dream for him is for him and his greatness and that he continues on the right path. We need people to dream that for us. Not to make it the shape or question that, but that he was there, he received, he's on the journey and that it's great to see more stepping up and now I don't have to be alone on the journey, you know?

Geraldine: You find people to step in line with you.

Kerrieanne: Yeah and I said, I can't do it alone. Come on now. All I'm doing is saying, light my fire. I'll light it on to you and then you can light it on to another and another and another and another, you know? Oh, light my fire. So that's what he's doing too is lighting my fire and he's made me feel good because he's feeling good, yeah? So we're all feeling good and it's like wow, there's hope in the world. There is hope for our children and I'm doing the best that I can. I'm doing 100 percent and I can see it moving. I can see us evolving. As my grandmother said, when she said, Kerrieanne, just remember us ancestors who are in the land. We don't look below, we look above. Don't forget that my darling.

It gets lonely, you know Geraldine? So when you meet a kindred spirit or you meet someone who is evolving to be that kindred spirit, then I get happy, you know? I get really happy and I just have total respect for everybody because my journey was to transcend a place that held me which was where I fit in to my little tribal section group and I moved past that. I continue to do that every day so that I can live and walk this Earth as a beautiful human being, you know? That has a rich and beautiful spirit. When I walk through life and through this Earth that I am able to just share that light and share that good spirit to those who I come in contact with.

Geraldine: Yeah. It's a very- it's a powerful gift. One that for those of us that have experienced something in similar lines to what you're talking of, Kerrieanne, it can sometimes be very frightening, but it's moving beyond that and seeing that we all have that gift. We just have to be open to it.

Kerrieanne: That's right. You're just like me, Geraldine. And I'm like you, you know?

Geraldine: Yeah, that's it.

Kerrieanne: In time. I'm a very old soul. I've been around. Just remember like I always tell people- don't get too serious, you know? Don't let life get too serious, because you know, Geraldine, I'll see you under that tree again because we'll have to do it again and again if we don't remember, okay?

Geraldine: Yeah, that's it. We've got to go back around.

Kerrieanne: Exactly. We'll be sitting under a tree again and I'll see you there, you know?

Geraldine: Yeah. It's true.

Kerrieanne: But for now, it's a great time. This is a time where we all have to step up because we need to as the energy increases and we're moving into the golden age. It requires us to transform to a higher frequency level. To be in this next age now in this dreaming of our greatness so we get to see the best of humanity because we're moving away- there is no tribalism. There is no such thing as racism. There's only one human race. What the Earth is doing for us at this time is it's bringing us back to that place where the one common interest- the one common thing that we all share on the brink of time is our place with country and our return to Mother Earth.

Geraldine: Yeah. We're already privileged to be a part of it and to see it develop.

Kerrieanne: That's right and we are all one. The water is a blood. The water is the spirit. Healing- living water- is the one that heals us, you know? That water it has no boundaries. E has no groups. E has no particular people that E favors on the planet. Water gives to all and it flows through each and every one of us which means that the blood that runs through you is the same blood that runs through me. That's the most exciting part, you know? Of where I am right now is the fact that I'm a part of everybody and that we're all children of the Earth, eh?

Geraldine: We're all trying to do the best we can.

Kerrieanne: That's right. She loves us equally, but she'll also deal with us too.

Geraldine: And give us reminders.

Kerrieanne: That's right. I know about that. Every now and then I get a little tap if I'm wandering off a little bit there. I know when the tap comes in, Kerrieanne, what are you doing? And because I'm so conscious of that, Geraldine, I can't trick it, you know?

Geraldine: Yeah, you can't just think, that's not happening.

Kerrieanne: Yeah, exactly. The forces know that. The Earth knows that. It's really, really important for us women now- it's important to allow that strong feminine energy now to enter and that's the thing Buddha that's what you call him, he understands now. I think he understands now. He has many forms. He travels with me everywhere this fellow. He's a being. He has many forms, but he is always with me. He'll appear every now and then. I met him again in New Caledonia as I was feeling a little bit down and I needed him to come and confirm the higher being. He was on my level to come and he came. We talked. He's confirmed everything that I knew that I needed to do for the next journey and last time I saw him was in Beagle Bay on the road to Beagle Bay. He was a hitchhiker. You wouldn't think, you know? That's why you've got to be careful not to judge people. He might look drunk, but he might be in disguise too, you know? It just totally depends on how open and true you are in that sense. He was there and I gave him a lift. He was right there with me. He never left me you know? When I was going through all that change in Beagle Bay and he just dropped in to see how I was doing. I have moments like that too. With the father.

Geraldine: Do you find that you can always live up to the expectation or is it sometimes not only reassuring to have the visit, but also to know that sometimes you might drop the ball for a little bit, but you can always pick it back up?

Kerrieanne: Certainly, because I don't really have anybody I can go to on that level where I need support sometimes and he drops in. It's funny because sometimes I'm not conscious of it or I find out that I had called on him, but not necessarily at that time. He just confirms everything I need to know at that time of my growing transformation. I asked him because I was seriously thinking about doing this government job for 12 or 18 months in Beagle Bay and we were talking and I said, no, I'll go to New Caledonia and I'll have a think about it. Whether it's right and then he comes. He was there and he said, you keep doing what you're doing and keep free and don't subject yourself to that. It was just confirming everything I needed to do because how you were saying, there are times that you can kind of be a little bit down and it's alright and you just need a bit of clarity and guidance and it comes at the right time, you know?

Geraldine: And it's okay to ask, too, for that clarity and guidance- like we can just ask and we get the help?

Kerrieanne: We get it constantly. That's why I always say to be careful what I ask for because it'll happen in that sense. And be careful what you promise. My sister reminded me that I sat on the steps one day when I was in Beagle Bay at the family house and we were talking about all the problems and the struggle and that things had to change and that enough was enough and I turned around and I got on my feet and I was inspired. I said, "in five years, I'm going to come back here and I'm going to clean this place up." Five years to that day is what I did, Geraldine. My sister reminded me of that. She said, Kerrieanne, you remember you made a promise five years ago? I said, "oh, tell me again?" She told me and it's really interesting. Amazing. I don't question those things. I never do that anymore. I'm very careful about those things.

Geraldine: Yeah, you just know it does happen and to trust it, but also to respect it. Kerrieanne, is there anything you'd like for other people to know about your journey that may help them in understanding how this flow comes to us?

Kerrieanne: Yeah, basically, you just have to express the truth in your own life. You have to stop whatever cycles you've been born into and stop the violations that could be happening to you in many forms and start to respect yourself. Don't give yourself second best, but the best. Continue to create a benchmark standard. Continue to grow every moment and enjoy the journey.

Geraldine: Thank you for speaking your truth and our truth today. It's been great. Very moving. I've got to tell you, the whole time that you've been speaking there's been quite this amazing sea breeze that's just been knocking bits and pieces through the house so there's been like a constant beat coming through as we've been talking.

Kerrieanne: Wow. It must be gorgeous.

Geraldine: It's been quite great to experience that. There's been a lot of movement since you've been speaking and there still is.

Kerrieanne: Well, Geraldine, I'd like to honor you and thank you for allowing me to express the beautiful spirit because I can't- I'm forbidden to write stuff and I would like to thank you from the bottom of my heart for allowing me to speak through you and share my story and that beautiful message. I wish you all the best with it all.

Kerrieanne: Yeah, it's really good to be at the mountain especially from when I was here last summer. I've changed heaps. Grown heaps and I'm on another different level now so it's really kind of good to sit above and gain high insight, eh?

Geraldine: Seems like just to go there, it seems like a very powerful place.

Kerrieanne: It is and just collecting more energy and I've definitely needed it, you know?

Kerrieanne: You've been in my spirit that way too.

Geraldine: I feel very privileged that I've been able to speak with you about such things. It's been very humbling to hear it, Kerrieanne.

Kerrieanne: It's a pleasure. Well, you take care of yourself Keep shining and keeping deadly.

Geraldine: I will do. Alright. See you, Kerrieanne.

> "One of the sayings in our country is Ubuntu - the essence of being human. Ubuntu speaks particularly about the fact that you can't exist as a human being in isolation. It speaks about our inter connectedness. You can't be human all by yourself, and when you have this quality - Ubuntu - you are known for your generosity. We think of ourselves far too frequently as just individuals, separated from one another, whereas you are connected and what you do affects the whole world. When you do well, it spreads out; it is for the whole of humanity." -
>
> Archbishop Desmond Tutu

Kerrianne Cox's Thoughts on Miracles

L - Limitless Power of Love and Light

L – LIMITLESS POWER OF LOVE AND LIGHT

> *"Give love and unconditional acceptance to those you encounter, and notice what happens."*
> *Wayne Dyer*

What is love? We often ponder on this question and anyone who grew up with Charles Shultz and Peanuts will know that "All You Need is Love, but a little chocolate now and then doesn't hurt either." Love is limitless and it is unconditional. We find love for ourselves and for all. Love is not manufactured; when we clear ourselves of our negativity, we are left with an overwhelming sense of peace and love. It doesn't mean that we won't find someone's behaviour annoying; it just means that the behaviour won't impact on us and we can extend our love to that thing or person. Love is at our essence and it is infused into that divine spark that drives us into the slipstream. We cannot give too much love because we have a limitless supply. We can tap into it and extend it to ourselves firstly and then find ways to extend that love to others. It may be in thinking of someone who is not well, in doing something for someone unexpectedly. It may be stopping your car and helping a native animal cross the road safely. It may be many things, but it is never wanting and it has the capacity to truly bring about changes in ourselves and in our world.

To me, love and light are one. In the last chapter, we talked about finding your centre and being the captain of your soul. When this happens, a natural flow on is to love all things unconditionally.

L – Limitless Power of Love and Light

Again, we get challenged on these things, we have the choice to move beyond the challenge and return to our centre and refocus on the love and light that is glowing. The divine spark allows the clear sense of our being to extend through us and into all things in our life. We begin to see that part in other people and look beyond the limit they may be setting themselves and those around them. When we begin to love unconditionally, we find that we receive more and more love and that also extends to the flow of the slipstream. We have a world opened to us that makes our day-to-day world a better place.

The laws of nature are also affected by love and light. Animals and plants respond to love and nurture and light.   There are no restrictions when we put love in our hearts. The love fills the gap we have left in working to eliminate emotions that no longer serve us. The clearer our heart and the more love that can be shared, the more responsive we are to others. Love allows us to forgive ourselves and others for anything that may previously, or in the future, affect us. It is not to say that we are not responsible for our actions and to love gives us a "Get out of Gaol Free" card, but rather love allows that place in all of us to radiate a new pattern. We begin to accept that all things are possible in this world. With love as our guide, we see that it is okay to believe in something bigger than ourselves, that love will find a way through the challenges that befall us. We also start to become the person that gives their best in all things and who truly is aware of the difference they can make, just by being present with another person and holding time with them in a state of unconditional love.

We find that it is frustrating to try and hold this position at first but, with practice and resolve, it becomes a natural and wonderful state that even our logical mind appreciates. For while it is important to find the place where love resides, it is equally important for your day to day living to have the balance that the logical mind provides, so that you can undertake your daily tasks. Our logical mind grounds us and enhances the realisation of the place that we are part of when love resides in us. Our logic guides our day to day living and, once we find a way that our mind sits with our feelings of unconditional love, then the balance created is the shift that brings the slipstream into our world.

That shift into the flow, however, is not always that simple. We are products of our past and this sometimes impacts on our future. Our past regrets and mistakes can hold us from our potential of loving unconditionally and it is really important to clear ourselves of these negative emotions and allow this clearing to return us to our centre. I have said before that when we centre, we find our divine spark. The two mix and meet to harness the flow of the slipstream that brings those miracles into our lives at a rate that we only thought was for the privileged few. The light of the divine spark somehow makes our very essence lighter. We don't feel as if we are weighed down with problems. We start to find solutions to matters that previously troubled us. We step into a world filled with light and endless possibilities and we find people are there to guide us and to participate in our successes and triumphs.

When we truly begin to love unconditionally, we find that we do not expect anything in return. It is enough for us to find that space within ourselves and recognise that every one of us contains that same potential. If we can harness this across families, across cities, and across countries, then we begin to see the shift in the world that makes way for a peaceful and prosperous place in which we can all dwell. Love that flows from us unconditionally usually returns to us many times over. We may not need that love immediately, but we find that it turns up at our doorstep in those times and places when we most need

L – Limitless Power of Love and Light

a hand. If God were to have an essence, the description of that essence would be love. Meeting God in that space of love, within our true nature, explodes the possibilities that lie before us to bring about the changes to bring peace within our immediate world but ultimately in our wider world. For if love is our true nature and is our essence, then at our very core God lights that divine spark for us. Clearing our centre allows our co-pilot, God, to help direct the flow of the slipstream into our world and we begin to see the results multiply and flow.

Why is it that we seem driven to connect with others in a way that brings love into our lives? We do this at a physical and emotional level but we fail to see that, at an unconditional level, we in fact enhance all aspects of our life. And the love of our partners, family and friends is only enhanced through loving unconditionally. We fulfil our greatest need of connecting with others through loving unconditionally. The trick here though is to love ourselves first. If we fail to bring this about, then we really are giving from an imbalanced and draining perspective. If we can find love for others, then we must be able to love ourselves unconditionally. Loving ourselves is perhaps the most difficult step of all in bringing the slipstream into our lives. We find excuses and ways to put ourselves down, we find ways to find comparison with someone that we believe has more to give than us or is smarter, prettier, or earns more money. What we don't realise is that person may be saying "if only I was more like so and so and look how easily they can do things and I wish I was as smart as them." When you find those things in other people, then you also find those things in yourself. So start loving yourself unconditionally. Take the time to find all the positive qualities that you possess and you will be amazed how you will find love for yourself and all the wonderful things you have done to date. If you think your list is a little small, then set about doing the things you admire in others. Set the goals for yourself that will bring about the changes in you so that you love yourself unconditionally and, in turn, you are able to bring that to other people and places. The consistency is to love ourselves first, find that our needs are met and then go forward and help others do the same.

We often lament our past mistakes and this holds us in the patterns from which we are trying to free ourselves. These patterns become entrenched in our lives and the flow of life seems removed from us. When we forgive ourselves for these past mistakes, we again allow that flow to shift a gear and direct things to us. The regrets of past mistakes no longer hold us and we move into the slipstream where miracles begin to enter our world. This is also true of forgiving others for their contribution in our life, even when we don't view the contributions to be positive ones. The exchange of life experience with another person only serves to help us do things the way we want to in the future, so that we don't make a similar mistake or error in judgment. So it is important to forgive the other person and thank them so that you can truly move forward. In doing so, you truly are displaying that unconditional love lives at your very essence.

Once you start to do this, you can begin to find this space easily in all situations that you face in your present and into your future. When you have the balance at your centre and the unconditional love that flows from this place, you find that attitude of gratitude transcends the problems and allows you to deal with the situation in a calm and reasonable manner. Love begins to drive your motivation in things and this in turn opens doors that were once closed to you.

When you come from a place of unconditional love, you begin to find forgiveness as a first place, not one that comes up after you have reacted to the person. This allows you to deal with any

L – Limitless Power of Love and Light

situation in such a way that you can respect yourself and the other person, even though they may be challenging you in some way. To react to a person with this level of reflection and respect invokes the compassion that extends from loving unconditionally. I am always in awe of the parents, or partners, of people who openly declare forgiveness in tragic circumstances where they have lost their loved one through a careless or intentional act. For me, that is unconditional love in action. It allows the healing not just for the family of the loved one, but also for the people connected to the other person, or persons, involved.

The true sense of unconditional love is not contrived, nor benign. It is felt as warmth in the heart that permeates through all senses and flows effortlessly from one person to another. It is invoked in an instant and it gives peace to you and those around you. When you find this place in your life, you realise that it is never too late to start living a loving and compassionate life. Even when those moments of darkness descend, love and peace often find their way to you so quickly that you almost are embarrassed for your doubt. Step into nature if you can and find a place to call on love. Find that peace in your day every day and you will find the slipstream of miracles waiting at your door. Whatever reason for your tears, your feelings of unworthiness, all these matter little when love is in your heart. When you truly open your centre and the light floods in and through you, then you begin to see how mountains can be moved and how we all can experience a greater sense of peace in our world.

ACTION STEPS:

1. Let go of negative emotions – really work at reducing their hold.
2. Forgive yourself for past mistakes and troubles.
3. Look for the love in all people; look beyond the façade they present.
4. Write out a statement that resonates for you and find time to read it every day – e.g. I am surrounded by love and light.

> "Life without love is like a tree without blossoms or fruit."

> "Love has no other desire but to fulfil itself. To melt and be like a running brook that sings its melody to the night. To wake at dawn with a winged heart and give thanks for another day of loving." Kahlil Gibran

L – Limitless Power of Love and Light

Marie and Vincent Ang's Thoughts on Miracles

MARIE AND VINCENT ANG'S THOUGHTS ON MIRACLES

Marie is a successful businesswoman who has mastered personality profiling. Vincent is currently writing a book about money. Both have experienced miracles in their own lives.

Vince:

A miracle is something I would describe as an unusual event that surpasses human understanding, logic or science.

It is often extraordinary, beyond normal expectations, unbelievable and in many ways, supernatural. Miracles have positive results and outcomes and often build and affirm the faith of someone who believes in them or can turn a skeptic into a believer.

I believe a miracle is something that is supernatural and divine. It is an event influenced by a higher power, uncontrollable by man or machine and it brings incredible blessings, relief and joy to the person receiving it.

Marie:

For me, a miracle is an extraordinary act of God. For me as a Christian, miracles are divine intervention.

Vince:

Based on my strong Christian faith, I believe that true miracles can only come from one source and that source is from God. That is my personal belief.

Marie and Vincent Ang's Thoughts on Miracles

Marie:

Same thing goes for me.

Vince:

I've got an incredible story that I would like to share with you. Every time I share this story with anyone, it still brings goose bumps and a chill up my spine. I feel it because I have experienced this and I can't explain it!

Miracles started coming into my life after I became a born again Christian in 1977, at the tender age of 10. It started when I suffered a debilitating illness.

I was diagnosed with a kidney condition called acute nephritis. People in the medical field will recognize that this as a form of kidney disease where the kidney's function is impaired or damaged. Because the kidneys were not functioning properly, the waste products and fluid started to build up in my body.

As I was unable to get rid of excess fluid and waste product, my body began to swell up from the water retention and the waste circulating in my body was starting to poison me internally. I remember hurting very badly.

My mum, a nurse became very concerned as it happened so quickly and took me to see the family doctor. I was immediately hospitalized for further observation. Further tests revealed the condition to be a lot more serious. I was starting to pass out blood instead of urine whenever I could discharge fluid. I was also running a high temperature.

The doctors were disheartened by my deteriorating condition and told my parents to prepare for the worst. There were really 3 ways that this could end up. Either I could end up with permanently dysfunctional kidneys which mean medical treatment and dialysis treatment for life, get a kidney transplant or I could poison myself internally and die.

This was in 1977 and medical science wasn't really that advanced at that stage and knowledge about this disease was limited.

I was hospitalized and studied by medical doctors and medical professors alike, as my condition was quite unusual at that time. They took regular blood and urine samples and regulated my diet and fluid.

I noticed that the kids in the children ward I was in were all very ill. I remembered seeing a kid who had her head shaved because she had leukemia and was going through radiation therapy. I remember seeing another kid in a coma and never left the bed the whole time I was there. There was another with tubes and drips in his body. Even at that age, I understood that the ward was reserved for critically sick children.

Over a few days, I was able to get better and my condition improved. However, I was still retaining too much fluid and waste in my body.

It was during one of the evenings that I saw two young ladies who came into the children's ward at the hospital to spend time with the children. They were talking, playing, comforting and more surprising, praying with them. I was curious and wondered who they were related to.

When they came to my bed, they spent time with me and spoke to me about God and Jesus. They explained how God so loved the world that Jesus was sent to die for us and redeemed us from our sins. I later found out the bible verse was from John Chapter 3 Verse 16. They told me that God will listen to our prayers and answer them.

As a Taoist, similar to the Buddhist faith, I listened politely but didn't quite accept what they told me. However, what remained clear in my mind was that if I pray, Jesus will hear me and answer my prayers!

Later that evening, I closed my eyes and prayed, "God, Jesus, if You are real, heal me and make me well because I want to go home"

What happened in the next few days was simply incredible.

From that evening, my body started to rapidly get better. The doctors who were monitoring me saw the sudden change and put me in for more tests. The test results almost floored them. They were really excited how well I was healing. Things were returning to normal and my kidneys were functioning well and showing they were healthy and strong.

The doctors were surprised with the 180 degree turnaround in my health but not surprising; they had no explanation for what had happened.

Within a week of my simple prayer, I was discharged from the hospital.

The doctors however cautioned my happy parents that it was more than likely that I would be on some form of medication for life, have to restrict my physical activities, be on a low salt diet and that my condition can reverse and I could suffer a relapse.

To cut a long story short. I am now 44 years of age, 34 years since I had been discharged from hospital with the disease. I have been through military service with lots of physical exertions; I have used no long term medication for my kidney condition for the past 30 years; I live on a normal diet and have not suffered a relapse even once! It is as though my kidneys had never suffered a trauma.

Do I consider that a miracle? A resounding YES! It was common for people in the 1970's with kidney disease to suffer a life on dialysis or even die from complications.

This would be my greatest miracle. More importantly, I knew I was given another chance in life, a chance to do something worthy and significant with the life that was returned to me.

Marie:

My miracle happened back in 1994 in Perth, Western Australia. Vince and I got married and this incident happened 3 days after my wedding.

I drove home after visiting my parents in their hotel. They had come to Perth to attend my wedding. I drove home alone, along a dark and windy country road. I was very familiar with this road as I had driven on this road many times before.

That night I was driving a little faster than usual as I was tired and wanted to get home to pack for my honeymoon back to Singapore the next day. I must have lost my concentration for a split second and the left wheels of the car clipped the roadside curb.

Once the wheels hit the kerb, the car started spinning out of control immediately and I screamed and tried my best to steer the car. I was terrified and didn't know what else to do or where the car was going to end up. I had a fleeting thought that I would end up dead.

The car crashed and I blacked out.

The next thing I remembered was someone calling my name and I awoke in a daze. Somehow, the seat became fully reclined and I was lying flat. I noticed that the lamp post which I had crashed into was about 2 inches away from me. I then realize that I was

Marie and Vincent Ang's Thoughts on Miracles

all alone and there was no one there. I didn't know whose voice I had heard calling my name.

I unbuckled the seat and somehow managed to get the car door opened and staggered out. By this time, several cars had stopped and concerned people were coming towards me. I looked back at the car and realized that the car had hit the lamp post so hard that it virtually wrapped itself around it. It was twisted around the lamp post almost like a ring.

I borrowed a satellite phone from someone who had stopped to help and called my husband to tell him about the accident. The police arrived shortly and I gave them my statement.

I kept looking back at the car and wondering how I managed to survive such a vicious crash. I had virtually walked out of the car without any serious injuries, whiplash, scratches or even a bruise! I shuddered when I thought that my life could have been cut short so suddenly.

Vince arrived shortly and he had this incredulous look when he saw the extent of the accident. He was very relieved that I was ok but he was also stunned that I had survived such a nasty accident. He kept looking at the car and back at me in total disbelief. The police and those who had stopped did too.

The car was written off due to the extent of the damage!

I went for a medical checkup the next day to ensure that I had not sustained any internal injuries and the doctor could not believe that I had been involved in an accident the previous night. There were no scratches or even a slight bruise to indicate the previous night's event.

I felt completely overwhelmed when I realized that I could have simply died that night.

I have a deep sense of gratefulness to a God who loved me and protected me from this accident. He had no only given me back my life but He had given my body back to me whole and untouched. I knew that my life was preserved for a reason and a higher purpose. I intend to fulfill that purpose.

This is my personal miracle and I will remember this for the rest of my life.

Marie:

I remember a miracle happening to a friend of mine in Perth. When handling a surgery knife, she accidentally sliced the blade into her thumb, suffering an unusually deep cut that required several stitches.

She was in constant pain and could not work or do any household chores.

When I saw her distress and pain, I asked if I could pray for her for God's healing. She agreed and we prayed together.

The next day, I got a really excited phone call from her. My friend told me that the pain was completely gone and when she removed the bandage, her thumb was restored fully. She simply could not believe her own eyes. There were no scars or even signs of the stitches!

That was a miracle!

Vince:

I recalled another incident. This happened to Marie probably three or four years ago. It was a weekend and we were relaxing on our sofa in the lounge and we took an afternoon nap. Marie was also doing some craft work earlier and left some of the stuff inside a box on the coffee table.

Marie and Vincent Ang's Thoughts on Miracles

When Marie roused from her nap, in her grogginess, she reached over her head to grab the eye drop bottle from the box to refresh her dry eyes and took instead, a similar sized bottle containing superglue, meant for her craftwork. When she placed the first drop in her left eye, she quickly realized what happened and woke me up and told me she had superglue in her eye. She was panicky and stressed.

My heart skipped a beat when I realized what she had said and I rushed her to the basin, telling her to keep her eye open the whole time with her fingers. At the sink, we ran water continuously over the eye while she tried prying her eyelid open, crying out in pain and anguish.

Between her waking me and rushing to the sink, it would have been at least 10 to 12 seconds. Superglue basically works in a couple of seconds and we were really concerned. Superglue is not forgiving and this could have turned out to be disastrous with permanent eye damage a real possibility.

I keep praying for God to intervene while we continued to run the water over her left eye I have never felt so much fear and pain in my life. My heart was pounding so hard and I just kept praying "Dear God, you have to help, please God, you have to do something, Please God, Please!"

It seems like hours but minutes later, Marie told me that she could actually feel her eyelid opening up and she could see. We kept the water running for a few minutes longer while thanking God for his intervention.

Marie eventually said, 'I think I am ok. I think I am ok." When I looked at her eye, it was very red but all traces of the glue seemed to have been washed away.

I am sure that God was looking after us that day. I honestly felt that without that direct divine intervention, things would have turned out to be a lot worse. I remember distinctly that nothing actually happened for the first few minutes under the running water and she was having real trouble prying her eyelid open. It was not the water that opened Marie's eye. It was the hand of God.

I totally believe that what happened that day was a miracle

Marie had her eyes checked out by an optometrist a few days later and there were no sign of eye trauma.

Marie:

Frankly, it is not like we can 'feel' a miracle. However, you do feel a sense of peace when it happens.

Prior to any miracle or breakthrough, you will feel panicky, helpless and hopeless. When a miracle happens, all the negatives are instantly overturned to a positive! Everything becomes good instantly. You also feel this keenly in your spirit that all is well.

Vince:

For me, a miracle brings you a real sense of inner calmness and elation. A sense of serenity and knowing that whatever is happening, is actually happening because of a divine intervention.

You know in your heart you are being lovingly cared for and looked after. It's not something natural. It's something supernatural orchestrated by a higher being, for a positive outcome.

Marie:

I believe miracles happen every day to believers and non-believers. Something as simple as waking up in the morning and the sun rising is a miracle in itself.

Marie and Vincent Ang's Thoughts on Miracles

The truth is people can't conjure miracles. Miracles are totally unexpected and divine.

Vince:

I believe that miracles do happen as a result of prayers. Sometimes when you have a need and you pray for a breakthrough, a miracle happens!

I have known cases where people have been healed from illnesses like cancer through prayer and intercession.

When Marie said that a miracle is truly an intervention from a higher being, in our mind, we know that it is from God.

Marie:

There was a lovely lady Vince and I got connected to via Twitter. Rene lived in the United States with her thirteen year old daughter, Tiffany.

One morning, I received a Twitter message from her informing me that her daughter had been hospitalized and no one knew what the problem was. The message was received at 7:30am Sydney, Australian time.

I immediately send a request for prayer broadcast to my Twitter friends. Tweets started coming back confirming that people were responding to this prayer requests. Even people whom I have never directly messaged to started confirming they were praying for Rene and Tiffany, total strangers to them. It was very heartening to see the care and love people can have for people they don't even know.

At about 8:30am, Rene tweeted and informed me that her 13 year old daughter had a stroke! I sent another broadcast Tweet to pray for a miracle.

At 12 noon, Rene was frantic and told me that her daughter had gone into a coma. I comforted her by letting her know that there were a large group of people praying for her daughter's health.

At 4:30pm, my friend posted on her Facebook account that she is over the moon and absolutely elated!

I did not know at that time what it was but I thought it must be that her daughter had stabilized and was recovering. We continued praying for her daughter.

To my utter delight, I received a message from her daughter, Tiffany at 7:30pm. She had come out of the coma with no permanent damage! Wow!

All this happened within a span of twelve hours and it made me believe that when we pray and solicit the prayers of others, miracles can happen to non-believers too.

Personally, I believe God does and will answer prayers. It doesn't matter if you're a Christian or a non-Christian, it says in the Bible that we are all His children, He will answer our prayers when we ask Him with the right motives.

Vince:

I believe very strongly that miracles come from an execution of faith. People without faith don't believe and because of their unbelief, things don't happen for them. This works in the secular world as well, if a person doesn't believe they will be successful, they won't!

It is human nature for people to want to see in order to believe. Sometimes things work in reverse. Miracles do.

Sometimes we have to first believe that a miracle is possible before we can experience or see it. In Marie's story about Rene,

Marie and Vincent Ang's Thoughts on Miracles

we visualized and believed in Tiffany's healing before it actually came to pass.

Being able to believe in faith without seeing is probably one of the greatest strengths we can have.

Vince:

Pure coincidence or a miracle? For Marie and me, it is definitely a miracle.

Quite a number of years ago, Marie and I were going through some serious financial challenges. It was also during this time that we decided to make a commitment to tithe ten percent of our income to God, through the church we were attending. We did this in obedience to His word in the Bible.

Now technically, by giving money away that we could not afford would result in us going backwards financially, since our budget was in the negative each month. Surprisingly, we always seemed to have just enough for our basic needs. At one point, we were living on rice and soy sauce but we never really went hungry.

We experienced two incredible incidents; an uncanny providence that made a huge difference in our lives at that time.

We were driving a 14 year old Mitsubishi Lancer during those lean years. The car wasn't exactly new and because we tithed our income, we couldn't afford to service the car. We ran the car for two years without a single service. I think I may have topped up the engine oil maybe once!

When things started to turn around financially for us, we decided to put the car in for a service. We were anxious about the condition of the car and the potential repair bills after 2 years without a service.

After the mechanic finished the service, we read the report and could not believe what we read. The car was in perfect condition! There was nothing to repair.

Vince:

It was quite incredible. Things uncared for will deteriorate over time. To have a fourteen year old car in perfect condition after two years without a service is pretty amazing.

Another incident I can think of was with a particular credit card company. We owed quite a lot of money to them and our interest payments were very high each month.

This credit card company was running an internal promotion for its existing customers. They were doing ballot draws and lucky recipients would get a month free from making any payments. They called it the "interest free month".

We were quite surprised when we got a letter congratulating us for being the winners for an interest free month. This helped us a lot financially and it was an incredible feeling being picked as a winner among tens of thousands of others. If you have ever won a prize, you will know what I mean.

Marie and I were absolutely gob smacked when we received a second letter the following month informing us that we had won the "interest free month" again!

Once maybe extremely lucky; twice? Winning this ballot twice in a row was absolutely unheard of! We don't believe it was human error as the ballot was drawn on different dates. For us, it was a miracle through a divine intervention.

Was a pure coincidence? In our hearts and mind, we firmly believed it was not.

Marie and Vincent Ang's Thoughts on Miracles

Marie:

Another miracle I recall happened about eight years ago.

A friend of ours told us that her daughter was pregnant. The good news was shattered when during one of the ultra sound scans, the scan revealed that the baby did not have kidneys.

The doctor told the parents that they would continue to monitor the situation for another month and if the scan still showed no progress in the kidney development, they would seriously ask them to consider an abortion. The doctor also told them if they decided to carry the baby through to full term, it would not survive more than 2 hours.

The parents being staunch Christians decided to carry the baby to full term. They firmly believed that children are a gift from God and taking that life through an abortion is denying the baby a chance to live. For them, it was also killing that gift from God.

Each time and until the last few weeks before birth, the ultra sound scans results remained the same — the baby still did not have kidneys.

The day of the birth was filled with both joy and sadness.

They had already arranged for a funeral. My friend's daughter and her husband spent as much time as possible with their new born baby girl and after a little while, the doctor came to take the baby away for a check up.

Suddenly there was a flurry of activities and excitement in the air, the doctor came in and showed my friends an x-ray. There on the x-ray was their baby girl and she had 2 little pea size kidneys! God in all His mercy and grace formed 2 little kidneys for this little angel!

For them, this was a life changing miracle. Their prayers, their tears and their hurt had been heard and God had given them a miracle. It was an awesome miracle that defies all logic and science. Still today, the parents keep the scans of their baby girl without the kidneys and the scan when God made the kidneys for their daughter.

I personally had the privilege of meeting this miracle baby myself years ago and she was the happiest baby girl I have ever seen. I remembered holding this little miracle baby in my arms and I was so totally overwhelmed that I cried.

I felt God became real that day and I have touched Him in a way…

Vince:

I'd like to finish for us by saying that for Marie and me, we see a miracle as a divine intervention, a supernatural event.

However, for a lot of other people, a miracle could be something that happens that drastically changes their lives. For some, a miracle does not have to be a divine intervention. That is ok with us and we accept that. Everyone will have a different view of what is a miracle.

That said, I believe that people can make controlled events or "miracles" happen in their lives, but they have to be prepared to take action.

If some one will take the appropriate action and work hard, they too can lead a life full of blessings, happiness and fulfillment.

By acting in faith and doing things others would not do, they will go towards the fulfillment of that faith.

I want to leave you with this thought from Helen Keller, am amazing Author and Educator who was both blind and deaf but made an incredible impact on millions of lives with her writing and poems:

"When we do the best that we can, we never know what miracle is wrought in our life, or in the life of another"

E - Emotional Mastery

E – EMOTIONAL MASTERY

> *"I have found that the greatest degree of inner tranquillity comes from the development of love and compassion. The more we care for the happiness of others, the greater is our own sense of well-being. Cultivating a close, warm-hearted feeling for others automatically puts the mind at ease. It is the ultimate source of success in life."* Dalai Lama

One of the last steps we talk about is also another important one. Mastering the way we react, or rather not reacting, to things is really a life changer. It is one of the areas in which I have most struggled and one in which I never stop learning. Much of my recent learning came from the Beyond Success workshops I undertook as a trainee coach. Now just when I thought I was getting the hang of my emotions, everything suddenly got turned upside down by me. This proved to be the making of my developing further understandings about my emotions and how best to manage and enliven them. The biggest thing to remember is that, just like people, the slipstream of miracles tends to bypass negativity. Now that is not to say that you can't recognise and acknowledge those feelings, but you just can't let those feelings control you. Many of us have read about the studies conducted by Masaru Emoto about the effect of positive and negative emotions on water. These studies could really be relevant to all aspects of our life.

As children, we seem encoded with a DNA pattern that registers our joy and our happiness and sometimes our anger and our fear. Most of us seem to have the scale tipped in either direction and then we work at finding the balance throughout our adult years. The data that we initially are encoded with can sometimes get jumbled by our environment and by our peers, by our families, but ultimately we are the driver. The input that occurs has effects on us, but the output is totally our responsibility. When we talk about our emotions, we begin to realise that our reactions to things tend to affect our outcomes. Harnessing this aspect of our lives is tricky and it really helps to have people who know how best to assist you in wandering through this world. Leaders in your spiritual community, self development courses, and other associated workshops all help to allow us to return to a state of balance and emotional mastery.

When we truly begin to express ourselves, we find that state of balance. In the state of balance, we begin to truly feel how something or someone affects us. This feeling is actually okay. If we are angry, sad, happy, or frightened, to be able to feel and express the emotion is really healthy. The more we can do this about things that are occurring to us on a daily basis, the more we can do it for things that may have happened to us years ago which still constrain us somehow. It is not, however, about blame or threats; it is about honestly and openly expressing how you feel about something. Sometimes you may do that just by writing it down and leaving it as a reminder to yourself. Other times you may feel the need to express the feeling directly to someone. That is when you need to follow a very simple premise; treat the person as you would want to be treated, but in terms that fit with their values. If we acknowledge this as our starting point, then hopefully any emotion can be expressed freely and without guilt or blame.

When we start to express ourselves openly and honestly, we find that we can relate better to people and them to us. We learn to pass on our new found peace and this enables others to mirror our behaviour and, perhaps, find a way through their reactionary cycle.

> "Do to others whatever you would like them to do to you. This is the essence of all that is taught in the law and the prophets."
> (Matthew 7:12)

The great question for many of us is whether there is more to our lives and to the world in which we live. Often the answers to that question seem hidden to us and we begin to give up on life because there seems no point to it or to anything else. When this happens, the person is at great risk of giving in and, in this state, they are open to make mistakes and to truly fall behind in things they are doing and achieving. Speaking from my own experience, it was at one point in my life that things just seemed to lack flow. My life had stagnated and everything was being affected. I had given up any hope of change and then something wonderful happened. A family member took me to Mary McKillop's chapel in North Sydney. I sat in a room and contemplated my life and what I wanted in my life. I really wanted contentment in myself and to find a partner who could love me and understand me. I felt a great sense of peace and relief just by being in the place. Call it a miracle or call it coincidence, but a few months later I met the man who I would later marry. At one of the lowest ebbs in my life, I found a way through and let go of the desperate emotions that were haunting me. The miracle that is my husband came into my

E – Emotional Mastery

life and brings constant miracles into my day. It took me to move beyond the feelings of hopelessness to find the gold that awaited me. It just happened to be in a place that gives off a natural peace. This in turn allowed me to move forward and find the greater purpose to my life.

> "And so I tell you, keep on asking, and you will receive what you ask for. Keep on seeking, and you will find. Keep on knocking, and the door will be opened to you. For everyone who asks, receives. Everyone who seeks, finds. And to everyone who knocks, the door will be opened." (Luke 11:9-10)

When we truly harness our emotions and learn to make an impact on life, not allowing the emotions to impact us, we begin to see the realisation of an awakening enlightenment. When we can take our ego out of the equation, our reactions to things come from a place where we are better able to place ourselves in the shoes of others and react to them as we would want people to react to us in similar circumstances. When we find our centre and begin to feel that in our daily life and in our waking existence, then we can begin to deal in a really honest way with those around us. We are all trying to learn and to grow and to prosper, but sometimes we actually forget this and that is often when the sidetrack comes in our lives. Being aware and listening to our emotional state and trying to find the balance in turn allows us to continue to find the slipstream in our life.

Emotional mastery has no boundaries in religion and it can be reached through quiet contemplation, through prayer, through mantras, through finding that inner centre, that peace that is waiting for us at our core. We are often subject to environmental factors which move our focus and can change our moods. As we begin to find our centre and settle our reaction to things, we find that this in turn allows us to have emotional mastery over anything that our lives may bring to us. That quiet contemplation allows us to find that space before we react or comment on things around us. When we live in that space, we open the opportunity to develop our emotions fully. We find that we can bring tangible results and bring about change for others around us. When we don't overreact to a situation, we can in fact diffuse something that would otherwise have become a big issue. When our ego interplays with others, we find that the road can sometimes become bogged down and won't allow us to progress as quickly as we would like.

When we begin to trust that our reaction and our emotions can be truly centred, then we begin to see the changes flow around us. We are all emotional beings and the more we are able to be present to our emotions and those of others, the more we can bring about change in our lives. Again we find this point at our centre. Now, a centre can be many things for people and it is important that you truly find the centre point that fits for you. Remembering to give thanks for all that you have, including the challenges, allows you to continue to move forward and become the person that you would like to be.

> *"Each one of them is Jesus in disguise."*
> *Mother Teresa*

E – Emotional Mastery

When we begin to find the space to allow our emotions to be honestly expressed, we also find that we are able to think more clearly about things, people and situations that we find ourselves in. We are able to react in a way that is most likely to provide a positive outcome for all. We find that we are also more easily able to find that dreamer in ourselves, the part of us that thinks of wonderful new achievements and innovative ideas, the part of us that becomes the catalyst for change in our world, and the wider community to which we belong. As we start to bring our emotions into a centre space, we are able to envisage the direction we truly want to take.

We have all heard of places and things being toxic. It is true that when we express negative emotions, we begin to feel that in our body and sometimes it manifests itself in a way that affects our general health and wellbeing. In the same way, when we place positive thoughts and emotions to our fore, we can feel so much better and more relaxed. Being positive also allows us to face those circumstances that challenge us in our everyday living. When we can find the neutral space, we are better able to deal with things as they arise and we stop making mountains out of molehills. When we instil joy and love as our reactions to things, then we truly find the slipstream flows to us and through our intentions.

> "God has been very good to me, for I never dwell upon anything wrong which a person has done, so as to remember it afterwards. If I do remember it, I always see some other virtue in that person." - Saint Teresa of Avila

Having mentioned the ego as being the thing that can intrude on our feelings, it is really important to recognise how we operate. Our ego will often override our best intentions and we find ourselves competing and feeling lesser about ourselves. We will also find that our ego will obscure events and people as they really are and will interpret them through the eyes of our ego and its template on the world. This interferes with finding our centre and also gaining that emotional mastery which is so important for us to continue our growth. Once this process of recognising our emotions and placing a stop gap in our reaction time, we find that we will need to practice and endure attempts by our ego to enforce the old way. If we find patience and allow continued perseverance to be our guide, then eventually we will overcome the need to place such importance on us and we begin to flow with the lives of others and the slipstream steps up to meet us.

When we gain the emotional mastery, or at least the development toward it, we find that we become more eager to improve ourselves. As this happens, there will be more and more circumstances and events that allow us to test and measure our own reaction to things and learn from the different outcomes each reaction brings. That reaction is not only external to us, as we will feel that reaction within our own being and that will make us feel great or make us feel lousy. We find that we begin to experience these feelings within our body and they guide the outcomes for our future. The eagerness to improve ourselves also allows us to be kind to ourselves when we find ourselves lacking in a certain place or situation.

The good thing to remember is that we are not alone in this part of our learning. Each and every person is here to discover this emotional mastery for themselves. As you place greater emphasis on it, you begin to see how others are doing, not to compete with them but rather to gauge how far you have come or perhaps how much further you have to reach it. Sometimes, a comment from others about the difference in our appearance, in our reactions, in our work, in our life is a fantastic reinforcement that we are improving. It allows us to look at our history in a similar situation and recognise that our reaction came from a place of power, not weakness; that we were able to empower someone else through our reaction or lack of reaction. It may only be a small thing, but this can bring about a huge change to us and for us.

As we start to regain our emotional mastery, we find our uniqueness. Whilst we are connected and involved with our fellow man, we are unique. When we set aside the reaction and find our peace, we see our ultimate potential and that is different for each of us. We harness the power of our purpose and we are guided to complete that purpose in our life. We are integrally connected to others and they in finding their own way are helping us on ours. I mentioned before that people will ebb and flow to our lives at times; the moment of the arrival and departure seems perfect when you begin to acknowledge the slipstream at work.

ACTION STEPS:

1. Practice not reacting to things.

2. Repeat step one.

3. Repeat step one.

"The healing is in the expression of the feeling."
Paul Blackburn

"Better by far you should forget and smile than you should remember and be sad."
Christina Rossetti
English poet (1830 - 1894)

E – Emotional Mastery

Tracey Fletcher's Thoughts on Miracles

TRACEY FLETCHER'S THOUGHTS ON MIRACLES

Tracey is a spiritual healer from the UK.

It is bizarre how I met Geraldine, as I don't go to the Angel of the North very often. I moved back to the Northeast of England about 18 months ago and it's somewhere I just love going. I've only been there about three or four times in the past 18 months. I just had that feeling that I had to go there that day. I have these pulls, as I call it. It's really hard to explain to you the pulls I get in my stomach, but I just recognize them now. To describe them is like feelings, that I now act upon and they never seem to let me down. There is always a reason I am drawn to things and it's usually to bring some light to a situation.

When I was driving home from York about three months ago, I had this feeling that I needed to go to the spiritual church. I started driving fast, knowing that I may not make it in time to their open circle. I just had this pull to get there; I got there in time and was able to stand up. I went and chose the lady that I needed to speak to. The message was clear and simple: she had things going on and that they would get better. Right now she couldn't see the light, but to keep her beliefs and believe in herself. There is more to a reading, but they are private to each person. At the end of my reading, her best friend turned around and said, "I am so glad you came tonight because this lady is burying her mum tomorrow and she didn't know how she was going to cope. So we brought her here, hoping that she was going to get a message to support her through tomorrow." I felt so humble to have been chosen to give words from spirit to her, giving her some comfort in her hour of need. So that was

Tracey Fletcher's Thoughts on Miracles

the pull when I was driving back from York: I had to go to the church, not knowing at this time I was going to give a reading. This is how it works for me.

I have had many things happen to me like that, I can't always explain them. I feel the spiritual world wants you to do things that you sometimes wouldn't think about.

To me, a miracle would be that you've been taken out of danger or somebody's been prevented from being killed, things like that; just where some good has come from a miracle and benefited people.

I'm not sure what makes something a miracle, call it a miracle, but it feels right and blessed at that time. Being at the right place at the right time is how I feel it happens. Sometimes a spirit guides you to a place. I've had two quite similar experiences, where there's been a pile up on the motorway and within the last mile of that accident, the feelings I got became stronger and stronger. When my children were about 18 months old, we were driving from Blandford to Morcambe and I'd had this feeling. I had wanted to pull off the motorway and every time I saw a service station sign, the feeling was getting stronger and stronger. My husband at the time missed the first services, then missed the second and I became really fearful. I said if he didn't stop, I would actually get out of the car on the motorway. It was totally irrational, I would never do something like that. So he pulled off the motorway at the next services, we got the children out of the car, they were only small at the time and we changed their nappies. As we were walking back to the restaurant, about five or ten minutes later, we heard all the sirens of the emergency services as there had been a major pile-up on the motorway. I felt stunned, knowing I had "the pull" not to stay on that road at that time. I was sad for those people involved, but many things have happened to me like this that I can't explain at the time.

It sometimes is an eerie feeling after the event, but now I understand it and say thank you to spirit. So I try to understand it more so I can help others avoid danger, or just to bring some tranquillity into their life.

Spirit sometimes sends me to places. I haven't got a clue why I've gone there, just had the feeling to go. I went to run a bed and breakfast in Devon last year for my friend so she could go on a course. I drove all the way to Devon, went to the bed and breakfast. I'd been there two days when I got a call to say the medium hadn't turned up at the local spiritual church. I've never done platform myself, like this, in my own right. I have usually practiced under the guidance of other mediums. I just went into the church and did a reading and I ended up giving readings to a full, packed church. I don't think I was ever meant to go there to just run that bed and breakfast. I feel I was there for other reasons. A medium eventually joined me on the platform, as she just arrived there, and it was lovely to have her support. We worked together well. There is no ego with spirit so there is no ego with us.

I don't know where miracles come from, they just seem to happen. I do believe miracles are given to us and it's how we perceive them. I believe they happen for a greater good and to benefit people, maybe from a higher source. I would say that miracles have happened to me. I've been fortunate enough to have my life saved a few times. A wheelbarrow once came off an open lorry driving in front of me while I was driving. It came straight towards my windscreen and bounced off. People could not believe it. I think my experiences are spiritually given. I don't know what other people say about miracles, but I know the three or four times that I've been saved, I know spirit has intervened. I feel how it works is that they take all the energy from around you, if that makes sense. They took the energy

Tracey Fletcher's Thoughts on Miracles

from around me. I never switched my engine off during the wheelbarrow incident but my satellite navigation suffered some kind of electrical interference. Spirit used the source of energy around me to help the wheelbarrow bounce off my windscreen. So that's how I think it works for me. Some people perceive miracles in their own way and believe it may be the hand of God, some people believe it's their faith. I don't know if we can possibly make things happen. I know for me, I don't ever try to make things happen. I just go to where I'm guided to and if I can help someone and make things better, I will. If I can't, then obviously, I can't. I do feel, with me, I'm guided by spirit and my loved ones.

Spirits are energy: they are spirit guides, tutors and loved ones who are in a spiritual place and still come back to communicate with us. I don't think it's a heaven or anything like that. I'm not sure how it all works, but from what I believe, it is when we die our bodies are like a vehicle and our spirit lives on. I've had a medium contact me before, who introduced me to other people, these other people have then opened doors for me, and this is how it works for me.

I just feel I am really looked after, like I said, pulling off motorways, guiding me to the right people. I think my life at the moment is very different from what it used to be.

I was a victim of domestic violence; this was quite a while ago. After this, I was married to a man in the army for eighteen years. When I was married, I was fortunate enough to always have money. In the last two years, my life has been so different. I became severely ill. I had multiple blood clots on my left lung, fibroids and tumours in my stomach. I had to have a hysterectomy. Within this time, I lost my home, ended up leaving my job and moved from the area I lived in. I have also been diagnosed with rheumatoid arthritis. So, in this period of my life, I have had to reflect on the choices I had to make.

I used to feel while doing my counselling training, "How can you understand a client's perspective if you have not been in their position?" The people I am in contact with at the moment seem to have had their own personal circumstances and this is how I came to work with these people. I am still the same person who has the same beliefs. I actually see things a lot more clearly now. I've had huge life changes. The experiences I have had I look upon as a gift.

I've just started to work with domestic violence survivors and I'd like to do work around domestic violence and bullying in schools. I feel I have had to actually go through these situations to benefit other people. I'm going through this for others and not so much for me. I know my own mother doesn't understand this, but I do.

The pulls, I don't always know why I'm going to the places I do, like church, so the pulls don't actually say in my ear, "You're going to go to church and give this lady a reading." I just know that I have to go to that church or places at that time. It's quite nice. I don't always know why I'm going and I think that's what makes it so pure and so innocent not to be told the reasons and I'm just guided there.

Though this is always from a place of light, I believe we're all a universal energy and we're all connected to each other and if you can go and help somebody, well great. It's about working from the inner space and I feel spirit guide you to do things for other people. I do feel we're all connected in some way.

Spirit energies want to come back to communicate to tell their loved ones that they're okay now. Yes, maybe they did have a lot of pain or they lost weight. They may have been disfigured, whatever their scenario is. When they go up to the spirit world, they become an energy of light and they feel so much better.

Spirits just come back to confirm this with their loved ones on the Earth plane, who are still remembering the terrible time that quite a lot of people had before their passing. Everybody is connected to spirit. We are all spirit. Everybody has spirit within; it just depends if they're aware of it and if they want to work with this ability.

I believe that, until you actually have an incident or have been touched by spirit or there have been some life changes, some people just don't realise, so they are not aware of this. I don't think we should push this on people. I think there are enough people wanting to know about this and that they'll come and find you.

My kids are so used to me going to speak to someone in the car park, anywhere really, I don't know. Sometimes you touch people, some days you don't. But you're always loving and open to people to support them. I'm just a different cookie, as I call myself. I'm different from other people and I always felt very different as a child. Just like one of my sons, who has been seeing spirit since he could sit in his high chair, which was his first experience. Your emotions are heightened and you feel you know things when you're not sure where they are coming from, you're just aware of this and work with love.

I hated violence on the playground, even as a young child. I really, absolutely, dislike violence. It's like a knot in my stomach and I think this is why I've been involved with men who have domestic violence issues. I think that it's their lessons that they needed to learn and that's why I was with them. I know that's a strange way of looking at it, but that's how I look at it. It was to help their growth and to give me greater understanding of these situations.

Why I had gone to the Angel that day, and met Geraldine with my camera, I haven't got a clue. They just send me to bizarre places, I meet people in the hospitals, I meet them in car parks. I talk to absolutely anybody. I think that's what it's about. It's about communication with people, isn't it? Spirits choose, with me, what I'm going to say to somebody and sometimes at that time I don't have a clue what I'm going to say, but seem to find the words.

I'm on an angel course in May with Jackie Newcomb, the big angel lady of the U.K., so that's really good. I was given her number by a friend and somebody put me on that course. I don't know where they're sending me next. I know I really want to go work in schools and shelters to work with domestic violence and bullying. I think it's great to stand up and think, "I've been there." I had my jaw broken, my face smashed, my nose broken, my cheekbone broken, ribs damaged, thumb damaged et cetera, but it can actually make you a stronger person eventually. These events in your life change your outlook and help you understand more. I think I've had to go through difficult circumstances, to help me know who I am and how I can help others to move on.

The love that I'm feeling from people at the moment; it's completely different, and I am not used to people wanting to do things for me. They're doing it because they want to and it's a very big learning curve for me, but I want to take this to other people. I once had the nice house, the nice car and everything. But I've got very little at the moment; my life has so changed that I am not materialistic. It's not about that. It's about what's inside and working with the light. That light always stays within us even when we can't see it.

When I was really poorly at the hospital, when I was having my epidural before my operation, the anaesthetist said, "Who are you talking to?" I said "Don't worry, I'm just talking to myself." I sat

Tracey Fletcher's Thoughts on Miracles

on the bed after the epidural and spirit told me "This operation is going to be bigger than you think." It should've been an hour and twenty minutes, but it was four hours and twenty minutes. Spirit said "You will be fine, but you need to get rid of some of the negative aspects in your life." This was a little pact I made with them. I said to spirit, "You bring my health back," (it's about 70 percent back right now) "and I'll be the medium you want me to be." I've promised that I'd walk through the doors that they open if they brought my health back and they did. That's how it's worked for me.

During the operation, I had an experience. I obviously got put to sleep, but when I came out I just knew that something had happened to me. I knew I had been somewhere light, but I don't know who I've seen, but I knew it wasn't family. When I came back and spoke to the doctor and I said to him, "My operation was a lot longer" and he said "Yes, it was four hours." I said, "I can't account for two hours and 30 minutes to about three hours and ten." He said, "Oh, yes, we had complications," something that I can't really remember as I was still spaced out. I think it was all touch and go for a little while. That was exactly when I knew, I didn't even know I was asleep, but I was aware that things were happening to my body and it was the angel energies that came to me, because I came back feeling and seeing outlines of angels and everything has changed since my operation. I see the image of them and if I put my hand over my ear, I can hear the chitter chatter.

I can hear the chitter chatter but I believe I have to really see it to believe it. I can't say to people, believe in angels when I don't actually understand it even myself. I just have these feelings that these are the angels. I'm off to some workshops to see if exactly what I'm feeling is correct and if it is this. I talk about angels. Everybody says "Oh, you're like an angel with your energies and touching people the way you do." I always joke, face of an angel.

I just want to stay pure to spirit. There are two words that I would like written on my headstone, and they would be "humble" and "karma". We should always be humble with people, regardless of who you are and where you come from. You should always help your fellow man. And karma, never do to people what you wouldn't want done to yourself. Those are my two words, I have nothing material wise, but I have so much love in my life and I've got amazing children. I have had about three or four miscarriages before I had my boys. They were triplets, but I lost one. I know one was my daughter; my son and I feel her, hear her and he sees her often. They weighed three pounds odd and they were born eight weeks early and you look at them now: they're six foot one and six foot two and only nearly 15. For me they are my miracles.

I was in Northern Ireland because my husband at the time was posted there, and I had lost so much weight. I was only nine stone something when I had the twins. The doctor said to me, "Alright, tomorrow we're going to have to put the drip in your neck or your toe because there's actually nowhere else in your body to put these drips," because I had been living off the drips feeding me for months. So I said to myself "I'm okay, I can deal with this," and went to bed crying and saying to my nana in spirit "Please let them hit the Earth plane. Please make sure they're okay. I'll do anything." I had gone to bed with my hand over my arm and when I got up in the morning, the consultant said, "Your arm has stopped the bruising and we can actually use those veins now. What did you use? Did you use aromatherapy or anything?" I said "no." He said, "Well, you did something to your arm. What did you do?" I said, "I fell asleep crying to my nana to make sure these babies hit the Earth plane" and he said, "Oh, you're talking about spiritual healing and I'm a Catholic. I don't really believe in that, but if it works for you, carry on." That was the first time I'd learned about healing and the source of it.

I am really fortunate that I've had these experiences from birth up until today. I still have these things that happen to me like this. I've just been at the right places and helped the right people at the right time. I must have had about 200 or 300 experiences and helped people within this. I won an award from Prince Michael of Kent for some of the charity work I've done. My thing is that I love people and I love life. Even though I'm having just a bit of a tough time at the moment health and financial wise, spirit has greater plans for me, I'm sure. If this is where I am meant to be for the rest of my life, then I'm alive and I've got people that love me in my life what else do I need, honestly?

I think it is important for people just to use their gut feelings. Just to work with what is inside. If you get a knowing feeling when you meet somebody or in a situation, that should tell you something is not right and look for the signs. That's really how spiritual things work. Always try to see the good in people. Don't get me wrong, you'll still get ripped off and there will still be negative people in the world, but people react and do things because they're hurting inside too. I try to always see the good inside the person and not what's on the outside. I know that doesn't always work, but that's just the way I work. Sometimes, you know that song by James Morrison, "I'm Just Undiscovered"? I think this is it with people. Sometimes we just don't realize who they are and they just need a bit of guidance sometimes.

"I'm not lost I'm just undiscovered, I keep it all locked up inside."
- James Morrison

I don't know about you, but I just love people. You'll also find when you work in the right light, people will just flock to you and they say to me "You make me feel relaxed, like I've known you forever." It's just your aura you give off. I don't think people love me; they just love the aura of who I present. The whole spiritual sense, it makes people comfortable and like they know you. I need to say to people, if this is what spirits are, this is what you can do. This is how it can make you feel. Asking angels for a cuddle at night time is lovely, a warm, not that all alone, feeling. I think feeling worthy of good things is something I am still coming to terms with myself. We all have our growth to learn too. I never understand why someone would want to do something nice for me. I often ask myself was I worthy of that, don't ask me for the answer to that.

My husband at the time was not always there because of the Army, but when he was here, he would cuddle me to sleep. So three years later, when you're not cuddled to sleep, I tell my angels to come and give me a hug because I really need that tonight.

I've been going through my reflexology and massage training at the moment because I want to be a healer. I would like to help people in a healing way because I want to work with teenage children who have behaviour problems. You give me a child who I can't get into his mind and I can get into him by touch, maybe. That was the reason why I wanted to do more healing, so I could say to a child who's really angry, "Give me your foot, give me your hand I bet I can make you feel better." Just giving him or her a different approach to life may help them refocus. I am a Reiki healer and the energies within this are amazing.

It is really hard sometimes to find the light in any situation. I think this is the toughest two or three years I've had in my whole life. My health is not great. I still have quite sick days. I'm on mega medication, injections and patches. My liver is slightly damaged too. But I have really good people in my life and I have two children who I absolutely adore. I am really fortunate if you look at it without the material side. I think that's what I need to teach to people. I couldn't teach that if I'm not in that space right now.

Things will get better; I do believe it has to. If you sit in negativity, you create negativity and this is what I want to teach to the world. We all can have negative situations, but you have got to look forward to the positive. Sometimes if you sit within that field of negativity you just can't see what's on the horizon. When you say things like "My life can't get any worse," then you'll find things do get worse. You need to try a different approach; it's going to get better. Then eventually things do get better. I'm not saying you're creating your own negativity but it isn't healthy to sit in it: you have to believe it will get better and then the people around you will believe. If it isn't getting any better, then you go and speak to people who will help you get back on track like professional people. And trust me, from my experience, there always is a way and someone worse off than yourself.

If I was ever fortunate enough to come into money, then I would use it to benefit others. Like when I went to Devon to run that bed and breakfast, I actually sat there and was given a vision. The vision I was given was I needed to get property of about a million pounds. I've drawn it on paper, it's absolutely beautiful. I want a healing centre and behavioural centre for teenage children and young adults, who have had a difficult time, deprivation and abuse in their lives. Give me a child for week, or ten days, at the centre where we have got cars and trucks to work on, they can throw things, they can get angry, let them express themselves. We can go swimming and just talk about life and show them a different spiritual way.

When I was at this bed and breakfast, I had drawn this plan of this centre. Anyway, this couple booked in and they come to the door and I said, "Hi hun, I'm Tracy," and the guy went as white as a sheet. They were nice people, the kind that had been through hard times in their lives. He said, "I dreamt of you a week ago," then he explained what had happened, I woke up and said, "Oh, Tracy, I'm trying to tell you something," his wife said, "Who the hell is Tracy?", and he called her hun, which he never does.

So when I came to the door and said "Hi hun I'm Tracy", he knew the vision was about me. So I told him what I wanted to do, if the spirit guides me to write books and do spiritual talks, to get myself known, to build these centres. Then I want the government to build twelve more. This is my focus. To cut a long story short the guy who came to the door is a plasterer and he takes children that nobody else will train as they have anger issues, and he always gets them to work alongside of him. He's had a bit of a hard life himself. He said to me, "Wow, what you're doing is what I've wanted to do. Let me manage your site for you. I've already found my managers, so I can carry on and do my inspirational talks and get twelve more. So whether I can get this off the ground before I die, or whether I leave this legacy for somebody else, I really don't know. I was given an idea and still wondering how to plan this, but its early days yet."

My kids are asking me "Why should I build a centre for people that you'll never own." It will be left to the trust, of whatever trust we're going to build. They said, "Mum, you're mad. You're going to leave millions to other people" and I replied "Yeah, that's why I'm here." That's my inspiration and that's why spirit brought me back. I don't tell a lot of people about it, because I just don't know if I can do this. I really want to, but I was inspired to tell you that and there we go. That's my little plan.

If spirit chose me to work for them, and help me financially to build this centre, then that's all well and good. If I can prove to the government that it is working and it's a great place and this is what we can do, wouldn't it be fantastic if the government could build twelve more? But life is life and at the moment, I have no idea which direction I am following. Apart from the fact I love people and life and want to work alongside them to bring great joy to people while they're here. So I still follow the pulls, and hope I can touch as many people and show them this incredible light and positive approach with spirit love.

S - Seven Steps to the Slipstream – Spirit

S – SEVEN STEPS TO THE SLIPSTREAM – SPIRIT

> *"Music is the mediator between the spiritual and the sensual life."*
> *-Ludwig von Beethoven*

When you started reading this book, you may have wondered where you would end up. In a way, we have ended at the beginning and back again. For the seven steps that you can undertake are very much like a spiral. At times they will be just a step away, whilst at other times you seem to need to go down a few layers and spin around a few times before you get the idea. That is no different when trying to connect to our spirit and God. Scientists believe our DNA is coded individually and yet there are similarities for us all. Our soul is unique to us but it is connected to the whole that is God or universal mind, the universe or infinite intelligence. Our spirit is true and waits for us to become integrated and whole.

If we look back on our lives to date, and go through the times that were hard, the times that were challenging and the times that were good and the times that were exceptional, we will find that we had an underlying strength. That strength never left us, we sometimes wondered why we needed the extra challenge but we overcame and we progressed. We did that through our own hope, our hope of better days, of continued beautiful days. We found it through our love of ourselves, of our partner, of our children, of our fellow man. Our trust may have been dented and tarnished at times but it was never lost; for trust and faith are powerful companions to love and hope; and they find their way to the surface of our consciousness and we rise above the past failures or disappointments.

> *"Where hope grows, miracles blossom."*
> *- Elna Rae*

In fact, these things are what made the saints extraordinary. Mary Mackillop kept proceeding and held her faith, even when she was excommunicated from the church that she loved and had served all her life. Saint Catherine died because she wanted to maintain her purity and would not compromise herself to anyone. Saint Francis of Assisi gave up his wealth and standing and helped those who could not help themselves. Their hope, their faith, their love and their trust all integrated to make them be the best they could be, to do the best they could do and to leave a lasting legacy for others. Their memory inspires people to have that same faith and miracles continue to flow. What about a grandmother from Windale who had such a great faith, such a great love, that she was cured miraculously and now continues to do wonderful work to help others? The saints and wise men who came before us serve as beacons and conduits for our own paths. The Bible says, in Matthew and Ephesians, that we are all saints. Indeed, we all have the capacity to bring the slipstream into our lives and to create a better world. We all have the capacity to inspire others and, in turn, to raise their lives. We are all able to let God's light shine through our being and show his love.

> "The heart that is generous and kind most resembles God."
> - Robert Burns

Not every miracle is planned and not every miracle is expected. As Paul Blackburn says, "That is the great thing about miracles - they just turn up." They can be spontaneous and this adds not only to their wonderful nature but also the great mysteriousness of it all. Miracles are absolutely a guaranteed part of our lives and each step we reinforce allows them to become more and more a part of our lives each and every day.

> *"The great lesson is that the sacred is in the ordinary, that it is to be found in one's daily life, in one's neighbors, friends, and family, in one's backyard."*
>
> *- Abraham Maslow*

What do you find uplifting in your life? What could become your heart song that makes the world seem a better place each day that you wake and observe your first breath? Find the signature tune that gets you out of the bed and into the day. It may be your family, your job, your plans, your partner, your friends, your career, your duty, your experiences. Whatever it is, note it and thank the day for allowing you to pursue your heart song again.

> *"Everyone in the whole wide world*
> *Has a special Heartsong.*
> *If you believe in magical, musical hearts,*
> *And if you believe you can be happy,*
> *Then you, too, will hear your song."*
>
> *© Matthew Joseph Thaddeus Stepanek*

When we set our mind, when we locate the infinite in our lives, when we reach for results that change our reality, we are beginning to see the slipstream in our lives. When we take on an attitude of gratitude, more things flow. Finding our way to our centre allows us to reach the limitless power of love and light and we master our emotions and each day becomes a new and beautiful thing. We find that our soul sings and that our life gravitates us towards fun and joy. We find that our baseline is set with these things in mind.

> "Knowledge is the fairest ornament of the Soul of Man."
> - Thomas Bray

When we truly begin to spiral this into our lives, for spirals do not just contract, spirals can also expand and do this simultaneously, we find that the steps to our spirit can be done in any order, at any time, with an ease that amazes. If we sit in solitude and contemplate we find love and light. We find our peace and we join in communion with the brotherhood that is man. In that communion, we find the slipstream flows through and beyond us. When we find ourselves buffered by the storms of life, we can rechart our course and move back into the slipstream that is God's creation. The ghost is in the machine and we are able to connect and convene our lives. It may sound complex, but watch a child and see the joy and excitement they create around them. Observe what they observe and find wonder in a flower, in an ant, in a rock.

If we are to find the secret, we couldn't start with a better place than unconditional love. In love, we find the companions of faith and trust. This is the holy grail of life and the flow of the slipstream; it is the trinity to bring about the slipstream into our everyday. Harness the enthusiasm that you felt as a child and place that into your everyday. You will begin to find others who agree with your ideas, others who support you and go out of their way to guide you. You find the world becomes that much smaller because you are that much more connected to everyone in it. If we can do this, if each and every one of us does this there is no more need for war. When we begin to sow the seeds of love, we begin to find that doors open for us and new horizons beckon. As you begin to share things with others, you allow not just yourself to prosper but others around you to do so also. You begin to allow them to see their own potential and they in turn can pass this on to someone else. The whole world then prospers with more and more of us entering that slipstream and surfing the waves.

We begin to find the synchronicity within our lives increases and that empowers us to achieve more and to acknowledge the wonders of life on earth. We find this is continually changing for us and that we begin by listening to those around us who already have entered that slipstream. They don't shout it, they talk and they nurture, they acknowledge and they share, they communicate and they enlighten, they care. We find that this is engaging and we begin to feel the flow and suddenly we notice that it is there constantly. If we are open we see symbols that act as our guides to move forward. These guides give us reference points in our daily life that allow us to recognise those miracles that are happening even when we don't acknowledge them.

> "I believe I can fly
> I believe I can touch the sky
> I think about it every night and day
> Spread my wings and fly away
> I believe I can soar
> I see me running through that open door
> I believe I can fly
> I believe I can fly
> I believe I can fly
>
> See I was on the verge of breaking down
> Sometimes silence can seem so loud
> There are miracles in life I must achieve
> But first I know it starts inside of me"
> - R Kelly

Sometimes we think that we cannot possibly achieve a goal in our life. Then, bit by bit, we edge closer to it and the doors begin to open and we see the possibility becoming a reality. Our subconscious is also a part of that whole: it connects the dots for us and makes the links that allow us to see the slipstream working in our lives. It links us to the whole and brings the things we need to our attention. Our belief allows us to see the truth and to find that faith in God, or whatever it is we choose to call our source of power.

We forget that we are special and that we are part of a network of specials. Everyone is special even if they have forgotten why, or how. We who acknowledge it in ourselves can also see it in others. Allowing us to remember our hope is allowing us to find our dreams.

Finding your spirit is easy. Allowing it to fly is inspiring. Can you remember when you felt light and felt free? Did you find it in the music that was playing? Did you find that in the dancing you were undertaking? Did you find it in the words you were reading? Did you find it in the peace you were feeling? When did you last feel your heart song and acknowledge your spirit, allowing it to exercise your movement in and towards the slipstream? These are your action steps for the chapter, harness the spirit and feel alive.

We started this chapter with a quote from Beethoven so let us end with a quote from Song of Joy:

"Come sing a song of joy, for peace shall come my brother.

Sing sing a song of joy for men shall love each other.

That day will come just as sure as hearts that are pure are hearts set free.

No man must stand alone with outstretched hands before 'him.

Reach out and take them in yours with love that endures for evermore.

Then sing a song of love for love and understanding"

S – Seven Steps to the Slipstream – Spirit

Profiles

PROFILES

PAUL BLACKBURN

Paul Blackburn has taught more than 100,000 people how to better their lives during his three decades as a success coach, counsellor, author, instructor and keynote speaker. Paul is the founder and chief instructor of Beyond Success, a training organisation that helps people to reach their personal and professional potential.

Paul's client list includes chief executives in ASX 200 companies, and his top 10 clients are worth more than $200m between them. Paul's down-to-earth style has been favoured by Olympic athletes, sales teams, educators and Australian Government departments, as well as the people who lost their homes in the 2003 Canberra bushfires.

Dozens of Paul's clients acknowledge him as the single most influential factor in their 'millionaire status', while hundreds more claim that the practices and concepts taught to them by Paul helped them to overcome terminal illness, infertility or depression. Paul's techniques also helped him recover from an aggressive cancer in 2003.

An inspiring speaker, Paul's audience size ranges up to six thousand, and his presentations are marked by their relevance, value and contagious energy. As one of his students noted, "It is not possible to listen to Paul and resist change.

Paul has the ability to inspire even the most negative person to change their life for the better."

Paul is also a successful author. After more than ten years in print, Paul's first book, Beyond Success, remains a best seller. Paul has built Australia's premier coaching business, all the while maintaining a strong marriage and a loving family life. Paul and his wife of 33 years, Mary, have two adult children and live on a property outside Canberra, Australia.

WWW.BEYONDSUCCESS.COM.AU

PAT MESITI

Pat Mesiti is a prosperity activist. He is a highly effective communicator and, most notably, an income acceleration coach. His passion is to EQUIP and EMPOWER individuals and businesses to experience growth and prosperity to its fullest potential. His expertise is to SHIFT MINDSETS AND TO BUILD BIGGER PEOPLE to produce results. Pat has spoken globally to some of the largest conferences, and his books and materials have sold over 2 million copies. Having built some of Australia's largest people organisations, Pat understands the power of harnessing people potential.

Pat was a keynote speaker at AREC (a large and prestigious real estate convention held annually in Australia). He has spoken at national conventions for LJ Hooker Australia, Century 21 Australia and New Zealand, Harcourts Australia and New Zealand, First National, Remax and Raine & Horne to name a few. Pat has taken four offices that he has closely worked with to No. 1 across various franchises. He has also toured the United States speaking to huge crowds for Amway, Internet Services and AFLAC.

Pat has spoken for and shared the platform globally with some of the worlds most influential speakers including Denis Waitely, Robert Kiyosaki, Mark Victor-Hansen, Jim Rohn, Charlie Tremendous Jones, Captain Jerry Coffey, Alan Pease, Bob Proctor, Willie Jolley and Morris Goodman the miracle man.

Pat is committed to taking people from being sales agents to millionaires. He will shift your mindset, touch your heart and increase your wealth.

Profiles

WWW.MESITI.COM

PAUL BARRATT

If you had met Paul Barratt a few years ago he was blue, puffing and out of breath.

Paul was born with a congenital heart defect and from a young age was told he wouldn't be around for long. But Paul is not the kind of person to lie down and die; in fact he has done the opposite with his life.

One of his greatest feats was in the face of being told his heart and lungs were failing him and if he didn't have a heart and lung transplant he would certainly die.

Paul heard and understood this information and looked at his options – to pack his bags, leave his family and friends and travel to the other side of Australia to await a heart and lung transplant, or stay in Perth.

Of course, he chose to stay but he also took up the challenge to be the first heart and lung transplant recipient in Perth, Western Australia. He spoke with doctors, health professionals and anyone else that would listen to inspire them to support his cause. Unbelievably, in 2005 he got his wish.

Since then Paul and his family, wife Joanne and son Chris, have volunteered tirelessly to promote and support vital charities, organisations and causes. Paul has been a Board member and advocate for the Heart & Lung Transplant Foundation WA Inc whose mission to ensure Perth people in need of a heart or lung transplant are able to have their transplant in their own state.

In support of various causes Paul has abseiled down city buildings, walked the City to Surf, walked from Cape Naturalist to Cape Leeuwin and even cycled 132km in the Menzies to Kalgoorlie bike ride with broken ribs to raise over $100,000 – he is amazing!

Paul currently serves as a board member of Heart Kids WA and in 2010 is project leader to raise awareness and funds for other charity projects.

Paul's next project is to Bike ride from Northam to Mundaring to raise awareness for organ donation and celebrate life with other transplant patients at a barbeque in Mundaring after the ride.

The biggest project planned so far this year is a fund raising bike ride on the Munda Biddi trail. This 498 km bike ride from Mundaring to Nannup is for respiratory health awareness (using healthy lungs) and to raise much needed funds for the Lung Institute of WA in support of patients' needs in Western Australia.

To add to this he is a Community Champion for Transplant Australia and a Local Hero Category Award Finalist for Western Australia in the Australian of the Year Awards 2008 who regularly speaks to groups about taking challenges on and never giving up.

He isn't blue anymore either, he is pink, healthy, has a full head of hair and exercises every day, plus he is a passionate advocate for organ donation.

Paul is a true hero and a shining example of what is possible after organ transplantation.

Paul is an IT consultant, Telecommunications consultant, Performance Consultant, Master Practitioner of Neuro-Linguistic Programming, Master Results Coach, Forex trader and Author.

He currently serves on the board of Heart Kids WA

Project Leader of the Munda Biddi Charity Ride 2010 for LIWA (Lung Institute of Western Australia)

Project Leader of the Kep Trail ride for organ donation awareness, transplant patients and the Heart Lung Transplant Foundation 2010

Project Leader for Circle For Life – making a difference in regional areas of Australia

Coordinator - OPERATION GOLDEN DRAGON – MAKING A DIFFERENCE IN THE WORLD

MICHAEL MIHALCIC

At age 36 I was diagnosed with lymphoma. That was September of 1997. My GP found a cancerous mass between my heart and my lungs and I was advised that surgery was too dangerous. The suggested treatment was 12 sessions of chemotherapy followed by radiotherapy.

About half way through chemo I developed an extremely high fever and was advised to go to the emergency department of my local hospital immediately. Needless to say things went downhill from there.

Within days I was in an induced coma, which lasted for a couple of weeks, followed by heavy sedation for the following week or so.

All in all I spent 3 months in hospital – one month in intensive care with a near death experience or two, a couple of weeks in the oncology ward where my doctors advised me that chemo and radiotherapy were no longer an option – it was too dangerous to continue with these treatments.

I then spent another 6 weeks in a rehabilitation hospital where I had to learn to walk and move my limbs all over again. You see, after not moving for 3 weeks during the drug induced coma/heavy sedation, I had muscular myopathy, which is when your muscles lose all strength and tone and you are left with virtually no mobility).

You'll be amazed at the phenomenon I discovered in hospital.

During my hospital stay, I discovered a very interesting thing. Lots of people around me were feeling sorry for themselves. And that was absolutely understandable! I'd done the same thing. You wouldn't be normal if you didn't feel sorry for yourself at some stage.

Anyway, I noticed some people got stuck in the "I feel sorry for myself" mode and weren't able to move forward from that spot - mentally. And because they were stuck in this mode of thinking they didn't really put 100%+ effort into recovering from cancer and getting their life back to normal. Now don't get me wrong, they wanted to recover, BUT they weren't even aware that their thoughts were sabotaging their recovery efforts. And sometimes the sabotage was enormous.

When I was able to eat again, I also discovered I had no real appetite for certain foods. Strange? Or was my body telling me something? I changed my food choices while I was in hospital. When I returned home my wife and I decided we would learn everything we could about real health and true nutrition. We had to discover why my appetite had changed.

My wife Barbara was wise enough to realize that, as she puts it, I was "my own best doctor", and never questioned my food choices. She set about discovering what a truly healthy diet consisted of and then implemented it.

We set about finding the best program we could for perfect health, and mental, emotional and physical issues all had to be included.

We then discovered true health retreats where naturopaths were advocating exactly what we had done over the prior few months and we've never looked back since.

After my hospital stay I would regularly see my GP every fortnight. Within a few short months he was amazed at the transformation that had taken place, considering I'd only had half the chemo, never started radiotherapy and almost died in hospital.

My doctor didn't believe that improving my mindset, diet and environment could have such a huge impact on my health. But he kept telling me to "keep doing what you're doing" because it was working, and working well.

CONTACT MICHAEL:
MICHAEL@MIRACLESORCOINCIDENCES.COM

KERRIEANNE COX

"I want to touch people with my songs, not just as an Aboriginal person, but as a human being."

Kerrianne Cox is an internationally renowned independent Aboriginal performing artist. Her signature song Beagle Bay Dreaming has brought her beloved home and country - Beagle Bay in the remote North West Kimberley region of Western Australia - into the hearts and minds of people all over the world.

"I'm deeply passionate about my music and the love that is created into form by music. For me, music is about healing and building bridges."

After winning the Next Big Thing Competition in 1996 when she was just 22 years of age, Kerrianne Cox said "I am here to inspire people in all I do".

In 1997 Kerrianne Cox was awarded a WAMi (Western Australia Music Industry) Award as Best Indigenous Artist of the Year and in 2000, NAIDOC's (National Aboriginal Independence Day of Celebration) Female Artist of the Year. In 2001 she received the Deadly Vibe Female Artist of the Year given by the National Aboriginal and Torres Strait Islander Music Awards (NAIDOC). In 2003 Kerrianne was awarded the Centenary Medal by the Australian government for service to her country. Also in 2003, Kerrianne was awarded the ALMA (Australian Live Music Awards) Songlines Indigenous Award, and was again nominated for Deadly Vibe Female Artist of the Year.

In Australia, Kerrianne Cox has performed all over the country including at major events such as the 2002 Message Stick at the Sorry Day concert at the Sydney Opera House, WOMADelaide 2003, season 4 of Outback Up front on ABC TV (Sydney), the Broome Cabaret production of the acclaimed musical Bran Nue

Dae, the Sydney Survival Concert '97, opening Perth Artrage in '98, Corroborree 2000, Sydney Mardi Gras 2002 and featured artist at the foot of the Sydney Harbour Bridge attended by over 100,000 people, as well as the Western Australia International Music Conference in 2003.

From 2000 to 2003, Kerrianne toured extensively throughout the United States and Canada, performing in prestigious venues such as the Kennedy Center in Washington, DC, the Lincoln Center in NY as well as touring in Vancouver, Portland, St. Louis and Seattle, and appearing at the Detroit Festival and the NEMO Conference in Boston.

In 2003 and 2004, Kerrianne toured in South Africa where she performed at the Awesome Africa Festival in Durban (2003) and was hosted by the Australian High Commission in Cape Town, Johannesburg and Pretoria (2004). She is the subject of a documentary, Trancing in Dreamtime (Fineline Productions) with the San Bushmen from the Kalahari in Botswana, that was released to great acclaim at the Durban International Film Festival in June, 2004.

Although she regularly conducts song writing workshops which heal, inspire and uplift diverse audiences, such as participants at the Kungka Conferences held at Uluru, Kerrianne Cox is more than a singer/songwriter. She is a catalyst for change and a leader. In October 2004, Kerrianne Cox was elected Chairperson of Beagle Bay Community by her people. "Now I find myself in a beautiful place where I am the Chairperson of my community and I can travel from time to time to perform select shows that I feel are important for what I stand for."

In 2005 Kerrianne was named National Artist of the Year (NAIDOC) and awarded the Yvonne Cohen Award for Creative Indigenous Youth.

Kerrianne's CD's include Just Wanna Move (1999) and Opening (2001). In 2005 she began recording her third CD - 'Return to Country' - about what it means to live and work from her home in the Kimberley. The CD was released at the International Dreaming Festival in June 2006.

WWW.KERRIANNECOX.COM

VINCENT ANG

Vincent Ang was originally born in Singapore but now lives with his wife, Marie in Sydney, Australia.

He is the author of the book, "Can YOU Handle the Truth?". It is about his personal financial journey from almost certain bankruptcy to being debt free within a few short years. In this book, he shares the key principles that enabled him to significantly turn his life around by using the right strategies and financial mind set.

Vincent has a true passion to share his knowledge of financial wisdom and help others take the journey of discovery to improve their own lives, break the chains of financial slavery and take control of their money. He has a website and blog that shares some of his thoughts and strategies to a healthier and wealthier future.

Website: http://www.vincent-ang.com

Twitter: Twitter.com/vincent_ang

Facebook: Facebook.com/vincent.yk.ang

MARIE ANG

Marie was born and educated in Singapore and she moved to Perth in Western Australia in the early 1990s.

Marie Ang is a personality profiler. She helps people discover who they really are by giving them a thorough understanding of their unique and individual personality and empowering them with the confidence to embrace life by leveraging on the strengths and working on the weaknesses of their personality.

Marie's interest in personality profiling started in 2000 after she read a book written by Florence Littauer called Personality Plus.

After struggling with her conflicting personalities which affected her self esteem, behaviour and confidence since childhood, Marie finally understood why she felt, behaved and thought the way she did. This "light bulb" revelation freed her from the emotional shackles of inferiority and ignited her passion to study and learn more about this subject.

Marie spent the next 10 years studying the different forms of personality profiling and associated programs dealing with human emotions. Despite the various systems explaining the complex human personality, she found that it all boils down to 4 basic personality groups.

With this knowledge, Marie was able to liberate herself from the expectations and limitations that other people placed on her, develop her unique personality and assertively design the future she wants.

Marie is currently living in Sydney Australia with her husband, Vincent Ang; author of the book, "Can YOU Handle the Truth?"

Website: http://www.marieang.com

Twitter: Twitter.com/marie_ang

Facebook: Facebook.com/marie.wl.ang

TRACY FLETCHER

Hi, my name is Tracy Fletcher I have been seeing spirit since I was a tiny child. I am now 42 years old, divorced and have twin boys nearly 15 years old.

I am a bereavement counselor and at college at the moment studying holistic therapies full time.

I am an only child and currently live in the north east of England, where I was originally born.

I am working with spirit on a daily basis and have had many experiences, which have touched my life and many others. This is why I am inspired to write about spirit and their influences on us.

Profiles

(The photo below was taken by me and if you note the light over the Angel's left shoulder, no idea how it got there. That's how I met Tracy and we kept in touch. Quite a miracle to see that light appear – no answers just amazing.)